What is Politics?

*Other **What is** . . .? books available*

Linguistics
Psychology
Communication Studies
Accounting
Social Anthropology
Engineering
Philosophy

What is Politics?

Bernard and Tom Crick

Edward Arnold

© Bernard and Tom Crick 1987

First published in Great Britain 1987 by
Edward Arnold (Publishers) Ltd, 41 Bedford Square, London
WC1B 3DQ

Edward Arnold (Australia) Pty Ltd, 80 Waverley Road, Caulfield
East, Victoria 3145, Australia

Edward Arnold, 3 East Read Street, Baltimore, Maryland 21202,
USA

British Library Cataloguing in Publication Data

Crick, Bernard
  What is Politics?
  1. Political science
  I. Title   II.   Crick, Tom
  320   JA66

  ISBN 0-7131-6504-9

Richard Clay plc, Bungay, Suffolk

Contents

Preface

What is Politics? is written specifically for this series as a guide to the nature of the subject, to the different ways it is taught and to some general considerations about how to choose where to study. It is meant as much for the intending applicant to higher education, whether at school or in adult education, who may be encountering the subject for the first time as for those doing something called Government or Politics for GCE A-Level or Modern Studies for 'Highers' in Scotland. It is intended to be both thought-provoking and useful. It is not a PR job for the political studies profession. A good guide will, indeed, be an enticement to some but a fair enough warning-off to others. I have written the main text as the retired old hand and Tom, as the recent graduate, has written the useful Appendices. But we have each read and edited the other's section.

While Tom reports on some existing and rather questionable attempts to assess the merits of different departments (and neither of us even mention one that had to be suppressed for fear of legal action – and a good job too), both of us agreed that it would be quite wrong to offer recommendations as if for hotels or restaurants – which in any case would have to be relative to your own expectations, and the 'best buy' at the price, as it were. The few glancing references to places in Chapter 7 are purely to give concrete examples of different house styles and imply nothing about merit, and are purely my responsibility from my own fairly wide but still limited experience. Only publishers' reps. have visited every department.

The entrance grades demanded are some rough and conventional measure of merit, but as Tom firmly reminds, such a measure of supply and demand is heavily affected by environmental and sometimes social factors. Nothing I could say about teaching methods and syllabuses would prevent many applicants making Oxford their first choice, nor make others sadly wonder why at Cambridge Politics is only a junior partner to Sociology. However, I have thought very hard about what I am now going to say, but I honestly cannot think of any department, to my knowledge, so bad that I would (in confidence) advise you to change your subject rather than accept their willing offer. Perhaps there is a lack of really great scholars, ambitious projects and new creative thoughts in British political studies at the moment. But many good books and learned articles are published each year and the average commitment to teaching is pretty high. Most places differ less than they perhaps should considering the scope and contentiousness of the subject. There's nothing like leather.

B.R.C.

1
Studying politics

Politics is the study of conflicts of interests and values that affect all of society and of how they can be conciliated. You cannot hope by study to set right 'this sorry scheme of things entire' but you will be studying something very relevant to the betterment of life in the modern world. Your degree will be seen as a *good* general qualification, quite as good from an employer's point of view (employment figures show) as any arts degree or any social science except Economics. Despite all the talk of vocational and technological needs, many big firms, looking for management potential, still prefer a good candidate with any good degree to someone perhaps over-specialized. You might as well study what interests you. You'll do best at what interests you most and the class of degree is very often more important than the subject!

What will you be letting yourself in for? Something rather different from what you may have studied at school, more wide-ranging and with more about theories and ideas. You might encounter, in different papers of course, questions like these:

'Is there a place for morality in world affairs?' 'How democratic is the American political system?' 'How important is social class in voting behaviour?' ' "To solve the problem you need to agree what the problem is." Discuss with relation to British government policies towards Northern Ireland.' 'How effective is sex discrimination legislation?' 'Is there such a thing as totalitarian government today? Was there ever?' 'Compare the powers of the Labour and the Conservative party leaders when in opposition.' 'Does the political philosophy of *either* Plato *or* Aristotle have any relevance today?' 'What justifications are there for censorship?' 'Did

Marx have one big idea or many little ones?' 'What are the main factors in political instability in Africa?' 'Discuss the relative political and military strengths of the Warsaw Pact and of NATO.' 'Is there a case for unilateral disarmament?'

Even the best of the school syllabuses are necessarily more narrow in scope. The very need to set and mark examinations creates the belief that there is a correct answer to each political question, whereas (as we will see) the main Western political tradition has been speculative ('what alternatives are there?') and analytical ('what are the implications of adhering to different ideologies?'). And you'll find that most university and polytechnic teachers of Politics are a pretty tolerant lot: so long as you know the relevant evidence, the counter-arguments, and can put a case well they hardly care what the case is.

A typical Politics degree or component of a degree will have some Political Thought, some Political Institutions and some linking topics. Typically the Political Thought will have both a course on the history of political ideas (often highlights of texts from the Greeks to the moderns, 'from Plato to NATO') and on modern concepts, or at least an analysis of the modern meaning of concepts like 'liberty', 'equality', 'justice' and 'order', as well as specifically modern concepts like 'ideology', 'party' and 'community'. Political Institutions will usually be divided into British and Foreign. All courses include British Government *and* Politics (though the mix of Government and Politics can vary greatly – a point to be watched); and most have something on the USA, commonly on the EEC and the USSR (different departments offer, of course, different specialities). International Relations is sometimes offered as an option in a Politics degree, and sometimes stands on its own or as a joint honours subject.

But linkages between ideas and institutions always occur and, as we will see, there are several different types of linkage. Some departments make Comparative Government not just a comparison or contrast between a small number of different countries, but a more ambitious attempt to see common factors in political institutions. This can take the form of a kind of political theory which also attempts to generalize about or simply to identify types of government and the general processes involved, usually known as 'Political Systems' or the 'Systems Approach'. And this can overlap with or pull apart from Political Sociology as the study of social factors that condition both political institutions and political ideas. This study can take both a Marxist form and an American behavioural or functionalist form. Strictly speaking, a study of the social conditioning of politics should be called 'The Sociology of Politics' and the term 'Political Sociology' would then indicate the study of how social structures can be changed by political action. But in practice the terms are usually interchangeable: only the most rigid Marxist believes that all political action is simply a product of social structure and social conditions; and only a dogmatic idealist believes that if we decide what is morally right then any desirable social change can be achieved, or prevented.

Almost all departments offer an option, some a compulsory course, on empirical methods of political investigation – mainly concerned with measuring voting behaviour and attitudes, sometimes trying to measure the intensity of conflicts. A few syllabuses still reflect a belief, more common a generation ago than today, that politics can be studied and explained scientifically (that is, statistically, subject to measurement and prediction), or that only those parts of it that can should be studied in universities. Partly there is now more interest in those aspects of the subject that cannot be studied in this way – theory and policy; and partly there is now a less rigid view of scientific method and a greater interest taken in the social responsibilities of science itself. Most of us now believe that 'facts and values' cannot be separated either in the real world or in the studies of the social sciences. The study of politics is inescapably political. The student must be committed, but to relevance not to a party dogma.

The typical department, then, doesn't just advance through 'ideas and institutions'; it will have a third column as well – although there is more dispute about the nature and name of this third column than about anything else. The subject is thus a flexible and open one. No departments offer syllabuses without substantial choice in them and few attempt to say that there is only *the one true way* to study Politics. The truth of the matter is that Politics is not a discipline if by discipline one means a subject defined by its own unique method; rather Politics is a problem area that draws on other disciplines, eclectically and parasitically.

So if you study Politics you will become aware of *historical* explanations of problems – how they arose; *philosophical* analysis – defining and refining the meanings and compatibility of concepts; *sociological* study – setting institutions and ideas into their social context; and at least a glimmer of *statistical* method, and of how to use statistics in policy-making. The student of politics uses different methods according to the problems involved. We do not reject problems because they do not fit a rigid idea of what the methods of a discipline are. Always we start with problems, and gather together whatever intellectual tools are necessary for the particular job at hand.

Names of departments vary greatly and sometimes reflect different views of the subject: Politics, Political Studies, Government, Political Science, Political Theory and Institutions, or, of course, International Relations. Most admission procedures give some credit to applicants who have taken A-Levels in the subject, but hardly any make it a rigid prerequisite and nearly all would take someone with a profile of better grades without Politics than lesser grades with Politics.

History and Economics are not merely good combinations with sixth-form Politics, but can be alternatives to it as an acceptable and sensible preparation for a Politics degree, especially when combined with English, Maths, a modern language or sometimes even Geography. A-Level Politics is a very good general subject. Everyone should be exposed to something like it while at school, for the sake of their political education, what some of us once called 'political literacy'. But you can study Politics at degree level without having taken it at A-Level and not be at any great disadvantage in admissions. Almost all first-year courses start from scratch and sometimes people who have taken the subject at school do less well in exams at the end of the first year than those coming to it fresh. This can be because sometimes British Government is taught unimaginatively as the introductory course, duplicating so much of the A-Level syllabuses that some think that they know it already, are mildly bored and sit waiting for the new and more exciting second- and third-year courses.

So we do not assume in this guide that you are already studying the subject. About half the students who take Politics for finals did not take it at A-Level. Indeed, very often students come up intending to take some other main subject or combination, choose Politics as a 'third subject' in a typical three- or four-subject first year, but then switch to Politics.

If you study Politics you'll be letting yourself in for a lot of reading and writing. Politics is like English or History in that respect. If you don't like reading widely and writing essays, or prefer a more directed, almost programmed, process of learning, then Politics is not for you, more likely Economics, Psychology, Geography or Law. Politics allows the student a lot of freedom to roam. It is an interesting, wide-ranging and attractive subject.

2

The nature of political activity

The word 'politics' refers both to the study of Politics and to the activity of politics. So first we should consider the nature of the activity. This will help show why the study itself can be so eclectic, disputatious but also compulsively interesting. The activity of politics arises from the basic human problem of diversity. That problem can, of course, also be a pleasure. Variety, it is said, is the spice of life. But variety and plurality can go too far, not merely so as to offend some people (some people will be offended by almost anything) but often to threaten social order. Wherever human societies of any degree of complexity exist the inhabitants will have some different interests and some different values. And people who might appear to a stranger to have much the same real interests will often differ in their perceptions of what their interests are, and people who pride themselves on sharing the same values will commonly differ on how best to attain or defend them.

Some call themselves 'realists' and say that politics is basically all about these differences, therefore about conflict. Others call themselves, or more often are called, 'idealists' and say that politics is basically about doing what is right. And a third school says that it is about reaching some consensus or agreement on the institutional conditions of peace and justice (how we can all decide what is best in the circumstances). But the mere fact that each of these viewpoints exists, and that not one can be reasoned out of existence, points towards a more objective and general understanding of the nature of politics: the conciliation and mediation of conflict in a manner widely accepted as just.

Realists differ about methods and moralists differ about ends, so through politics mankind must try to find acceptable compromises between differing values and interests. Even the harshest autocrats, if they are to survive, particularly if they are to ensure a reasonably peaceful succession, must be politically adept, make some compromises, however one-sided. Coercion can help but it can never do the whole job. Tyrants and super-heroes have to sleep, have to trust someone, have to rely on some loyalty. Think of all those mythic Philistine war-lords killed by some brave Judith in the night. The most absolute Roman Emperor had to keep the Praetorian guard especially happy. In Germanic languages 'true' has the additional meaning of 'trusty', as in 'true friend', and Nordic chieftains would often only trust their *treue hund*, trusty hound, to guard them when they slept.

So to say that 'politics is about power' is a melodramatic and misleading half-truth, if by power is simply meant coercion. Said Rousseau, 'the strongest is never strong enough to be always master, unless he transforms strength into right and obedience into duty.' Political power is always more than coercion. One of the greatest modern thinkers, Hannah Arendt, in her book *On Violence* (1970) defined power as 'acting in concert', acting together. Certainly the more people who can act together, the greater the power. And she said that violence, far from being an extension of political power, was actually the breakdown of political power. Violence witnesses the breakdown of both persuasion and the human habit of 'acting together' with mutual trust. War is *not*, then, as Karl von Clausewitz would have had us believe, 'the continuation of politics by other means'; rather, in a very real and terrible sense, it is its breakdown.

As well as *power* there is *authority*. It is only by authority that the few can rule the many and it is only by authority that the many can agree to delegate power so that decisions can be made in societies larger than primary or face-to-face small groups. Authority is the respect that people give to someone who can exercise some skill that they recognize as needed. All power needs to legitimize itself as authority. Authority by itself, like power, is neither good nor bad; it depends how it is used. People who say that they are against all authority more often mean, unless they are anarchists, that they are against authoritarianism. Authoritarianism means either the refusal of a legitimate authority to explain itself and offer reasons or, more often, the attempt by a person or body whose authority is recognized and earned in one sphere to generalize that into all other spheres.

In Dylan Thomas's *Under Milk Wood* old Captain Catt, blind and bedridden, suddenly cries while dreaming of the good old days – or rather of a quarrel in a brothel in some foreign port: 'Damn you, the mulatto woman, she's mine. Who's captain here?' Dramatically, the poet gives no answer. The scene changes. But the implication is clear. While old Catt's men would not have dared to cross him at sea, knowing and respecting his skill at keeping the old tub afloat on which all their lives and livelihoods depended, his authority was evidently not accepted as being transferable to recreational activities ashore. Doubtless such activities produce a different kind of captaincy.

So one way of looking at politics is as a constant attempt to turn *power* into *authority*, rulers trying always to extend it, citizens trying always to limit it. Historically those who wanted absolute power have always had to claim either to be God – for to be God, or absolutely good, is the only possible justification of absolute power; or at least to claim some special relationship with God – even Elizabeth Tudor had herself styled 'Christ's vicar in this realm of England'.

To go to the other extreme, some have pictured politics as nothing more than the assertion of popular power or democracy: true power must reside in the will of the people. But democracies cannot dispense with leadership and authority so long as they cannot dispense with order and government itself. We enjoy representative not direct democracy. Governments in democracies can keep their authority, however, only if they are democratically elected, have to face re-election periodically, allow considerable rights to their opponents and to the press, and do not get too far out of touch with public opinion. But who counts as 'the people' or 'the public', that is as citizens, has always been both greatly disputed and astonishingly narrow. We live in the first generations in which, in a minority of countries, women (who make up slightly more than half of humanity) are believed to have equal rights with men.

Another way of looking at the nature of politics is that mankind is involved in a constant dialectic or push and pull between *survival* and *justice*. Political philosophers have always stressed one of these rather than the other, but none have done so without some reservations or escape hatches. It is plain that there cannot be a just society unless there is an organized society to be just. In this sense 'order' is the primal concept of political life. It must come first, both logically and historically. Even the great radical reformer Jeremy Bentham said, 'Most men desire to be governed in a known way before they desire to be governed well'. Men can endure a regular oppression, or bad laws: but is hard to live sanely without order and law. So we can study different types of order, sometimes with remarkably little concern for their justice. Do they work (that is survive) at all? How do they work?

There is always a constant tension between 'Let justice be done though the heavens fall' (as is improbably carved over the Old Bailey criminal courts) and 'how can there be any justice if the walls of the city fall?' The primary functions of government were long described as 'the defence of the realm and the enforcement of the peace'. To those ends the powers of the king or the state were held to be absolute – but only for those ends. The late Harold Laski loved to quote *Isaiah*; 'Where there is no vision shall the people perish'; but one could easily reply, 'if there is no organized people, then visions are useless'. Or it is 'my country right or wrong' against 'my land is no land if the people walk not in the paths of righteousness'.

But we do not need to choose. Rather we should study which mood or theme is appropriate to which situation. 'Where the very safety of a country depends upon the resolution to be taken', said Machiavelli, 'no consideration of justice or injustice, humanity or cruelty, nor of glory or shame, should be allowed to prevail. But, putting all other considerations aside, the only question should be, "What course will save the life and liberty of the country?" ' *If* things have indeed come to that pass (the very safety of the state, not the convenience of a government or partisan interpretation of national interest), he is probaby right – for the duration of the emergency. That is Machiavelli of *The Prince*. But he also taught in *The Discourses* that the best way to preserve a state through time is to divide power in a republican manner, just as you need to concentrate it in an emergency. It is interesting to remember that 'dictator' originally meant a constitutional office in the

Roman Republic which could exercise the powers of the Senate and the tribunes of the people for the duration of an emergency. If a man held on to power beyond that, or fermented further emergencies to justify his retention of power, then he was deemed to be an outlaw, it was held to be the duty of patriots to kill him.

The greatest philosopher of survival at all costs was Thomas Hobbes, deeply affected by the English Civil War, especially when good and honest friends of his became divided in their opinions and were uselessly killed. One of them was Lucius Cary, Viscount Falkland, who served the king with deep misgivings. Clarendon in his *History of the Great Rebellion* described him sitting in the Royalist camp muttering the words 'Peace, Peace' and telling his friends that 'the very agony of war, . . . the calamities and desolation that the kingdom must and did endure, took his sleep from him and would shortly break his heart.' He rode into the Parliamentary lines in the battle at Newbury virtually committing suicide. Hobbes famously argued in his *Leviathan* that unless we surrender all political power to the state, the life of man will be 'solitary, poor, nasty, brutish and short'. Only by surrendering our natural powers can we radically diminish the chances of violent death, and hope to die in our beds rather than with our boots on. Otherwise it is as if we are in a state of nature, the *bellum omnes contra omnes*, 'the war of all against all'. 'The general inclination of mankind', said Hobbes, is 'a perpetual and restless desire of power after power, that ceaseth only in death.' And only an unlimited and superior power can prevent perpetual civil war, and all states must perpetually 'stand like armed gladiators against each other'.

Yet there is often more than meets the eye in such a logical but stark argument. Always look for the question that is really being answered. Quite what is it that is to be preserved at all costs? To Hobbes it is not the state, not the nation, not the clan, nor the dynasty, but the lives of *individuals*. We must surrender all power, but if the state fails to maintain the peace, if our lives become safer in the ranks of the enemy, then loyalty and obedience not merely cease but switch. The absolute state suddenly becomes desperately fragile at this vital point: if the fortunes of battle swing against the true king, then we simply, as a matter of rational self-interest, change sides. Not for

glories of
our blood
and state

Hobbes any heroics about loyalty, honour, or dying for the true or lost cause. So Hobbes provides a theory of a strong state, but strong only in order to preserve the lives of its inhabitants. He didn't expect the sovereign to do much except enforce the laws and keep the peace (more like Charles II than Adolf Hitler). He assumed a natural economic and social order that would be virtually self-regulating given an absolute guarantee of law and order – a view still held by Mrs Thatcher and others.

Machiavelli, as we've already seen, counsels a prince to stop at nothing to preserve a state, and also says that it needs a prince to create a republic out of unlikely human material (the rarest and greatest political act); yet in *The Prince* even he briefly slips in the argument that republics are better at preserving states through time. And in the *Discourses* he openly praises an idealized republic of Rome for being so strong due to its ability to trust the common people with arms; whereas so many autocrats spend half their time keeping arms out of the hands of their own people and half their money on unreliable mercenaries.

Machiavelli leads us right to the edge of the modern dilemmas of mass politics and hence of our subjects of study, speculation and reflection. 'The politics of the future', said Napoleon, 'will be the art of moving the masses.' Or, the other side of the coin, how do the new masses control their governments? Mass literacy both creates greater popular demands for controlling and directing government from beneath, and gives governments greater opportunities for 'moving the masses'. The modern popular press, for instance, is a two-edged sword. So there is another fundamental duality in the nature of politics, *government* and *consent*.

'All government rests on the consent of the governed', said the American rebels in 1776. But the matter is not as simple as they thought. For governments which can mobilize and influence the governed *en masse* can now be far stronger than old-fashioned autocracies which so much depended on passive obedience, on letting sleeping dogs lie, rather than on stirring things up. If the processes of giving consent to be governed become too elaborate, then the basic framework of order can be threatened on which consent and liberty themselves depend for survival. Abraham Lincoln shrewdly and sadly asked at the beginning of the American Civil War: 'Is there in all republics this inherent and fatal weakness? Must a government of necessity be too *strong* for the liberties of its people, or too weak to maintain its own existence?'

Both the practice and the study of politics has to embrace both the fact of government and the fact of consent. Any theory that asserts the one wholly at the expense of the other is either totally inadequate, or is bluffing. Hobbes was bluffing. He thought that consent in his day had gone too far, not really that any ruler could dispense with it. And the Americans of 1787 found a striking compromise in the new federal system between central and local power.

So politics, as the conservative Edmund Burke said, must be 'the art of the possible'. No sensible socialist should disagree with him, though conservatives and socialists will usually differ about what is possible as well as about what is desirable. This duality runs through the study of Politics (as we will soon see). The art of the possible, of whatever kind, must involve compromise. But all compromises are not of a kind. And there may be circumstances in which we can admire, praise and honour someone who refuses to compromise, but none the less accepts what is politically expedient.

Consider two graphic examples of compromise. One is from the First World War. Lord Beaverbrook wrote in his book *The Decline and Fall of Lloyd George* (1981):

He got nothing but hatred from the Generals who in that war fiercely opposed any civilian attempt to interfere with their strategy. Though Lloyd George had a deep and well-founded distrust of the Generals, his political instinct warned him that it would not be safe to go against popular idols such as Haig and Robertson. Consequently he could and would conspire against Haig and seek to undermine him, but he would not assert his authority and insist that the campaigns of slaughter must cease. He was and had to be the politician, the man who tried to gauge the current and not to go against it. Failure to heed that same current would have driven him from power.

Beaverbrook did not imply that Lloyd George was wrong to hang on to power, he implied that anyone who followed him would be even more unable to restrain the slaughtering generals.

The other example of compromise is from the Second World

War. President Franklin Roosevelt had embarked on a 'preparedness campaign' in 1940 but anti-war sentiment and radical as well as conservative isolationism were sweeping the campuses. In one of his typical personal attempts at influence he summoned the leader of the American Youth Congress to audience – as news of the German victory in France poured in. In *Roosevelt: the Lion and the Fox* (1956) James MacGregor Burns relates:

Speech after speech from the floor said that something serious seemed to have happened to the New Deal – the President was forgetting the first line of defence – social security, education, housing, food. Billions of dollars for armaments, but cuts in welfare legislation. It was not enough for the President to blame Congress, where was his leadership? Said one: 'We are very – shall I say sick? – yes, but at the same time, we are a little bit angry that the President and members of his cabinet have not carried this fight once again to the people!'

Roosevelt asked him if he had read Carl Sandburg's *Lincoln*? 'I think the impression was that Lincoln was a pretty sad man because he could not do all he wanted to to do at one time, and I think you will find examples where Lincoln had to compromise to get a little something. He had to compromise to make a few gains. Lincoln was one of those unfortunate people called a 'politician' but he was practical enough to get a great many things for his country. . . .'

Does it depend on motives, however, as well as results before one can be sure that a Roosevelt or a Lincoln was a great politician and not, like Lloyd George, despite Beaverbrook's special pleading, a timeserver? Presumably a true politician's compromises at least get 'a little something' better, whereas a timeserver just cleverly puts off problems which are then left for others to sort out later. Some seek activity in office, whilst others seek office alone.

Contradictions between the claims of individual conscience and the safety of the state are inevitable, as are those between individual rights and the general interest. That is inherent in the nature of political life. There are no general solutions. There are general principles but these principles themselves, like 'liberty', 'equality', 'justice', jostle for priority. We can only study their relevance, application and relative priorities in particular times and circumstances. The philosophical and the empirical aspects of the study must be put to work together, however much some syllabuses and some teachers try hard to keep them apart.

How closely we perceive the ways in which 'politics' is linked to practices of government can best be understood if, in the following two chapters, we offer a sketch of the origins and development of the tradition of political activity itself and then attempt to summarize how it applies to our modern understanding of what John Stuart Mill called in the title of a seminal book, '*Representative Government*'.

If you look at Mill's book, incidentally, you will see at once how misleading is the conventional division of the syllabus between Political Institutions and Political Thought. Of course, one cannot talk about everything at once. The subject has to be divided somehow, and some quite arbitrary divisions have to be made simply for convenience of study and teaching. Some of these divisions have little or no theoretical justification but have become so convenient and conventional that they are viewed as truths in themselves, rather than as particular ways of handling knowledge. So before we describe these conventional divisions of the cake in greater detail, bear with us if we talk about the baking and eating of the cake itself.

3

The origins of political life

Political thought and speculation originated in Europe just as science did. But they can both be applied and adapted everywhere. And every application proves different. Third World countries are no more threatening their own cultures by using 'Western politics' than they are by using Western science.

This may sound very 'Eurocentric'; but free-ranging speculation about what can be done through politics is, as far as we know, no older than the Greeks of the fifth century BC. Plato is the first person we know who, in his dialogues, drew a clear distinction between what is taught to us as established *law* and what we can find out by ourselves, by reasoning and debate, to be *justice*. A lot of teachers and textbooks go on about 'respecting the rule of law'. And so we should! But we should also ask whether particular laws are just, and, if not, how they can be changed.

Plato maintained that men could construct either (as in his dialogue *The Republic*) an ideal state, or (as in his dialogue *The Laws*) at least a better one. What is remarkable is that he distinguished between *law* and *justice* at all, that he broke from traditional morality to establish philosophy as a radical critique of tradition. If his conclusions are, to us, highly authoritarian, his method did put everything up for grabs and establish critical reasoning as part of politics and as a faculty or ability that can be possessed and exercised by people other than divine rulers, or rulers who claim to embody a divinely established social order.

How did political thinking and political activity arise? We don't really know. Possible answers are long and uncertain. But the contrast is vivid between the speculative Greeks, who recognized a variety of forms of government and society and believed that men should be citizens who could choose which to have, and the otherwise almost universal belief in the ancient world that there was a difference in nature between rulers and ruled and that this difference was part of divine order. And since rulers were themselves thought to be part of a preordained divine order, it was believed that they could make no fundamental changes. They may be skilful in battle or unlucky with the harvests but if there is no way of changing the order of things, then warfare and famines are endemic.

Aristotle was the founder of the study of politics as we know it. Five centuries before the beginning of the Christian era he made three basic assertions and one important assumption. Firstly, he asserted that man is naturally a social animal. He is born into social relationships and becomes himself at his best by interaction with others as a citizen, not by self-assertion or subservience. 'The man who thinks he can live outside the *polis* is either a beast or a god' – that is, to be self-sufficient or fully autonomous is not to be human. Secondly, he asserted that societies are composed of a variety of elements – he said that his teacher, Plato, was mistaken to believe that a *polis* (or city-state) without a single standard of righteousness or justice is unstable; rather Aristotle argues that any attempt to impose a single standard, rather than mediating and balancing existing elements, will cause it to fall apart. Thirdly, he asserted that the best possible form of government is 'mixed government' – neither monarchy, aristocracy or democracy (which he identified as basic forms) alone. Democracy is certainly to be preferred to the others, he says, if that is the only choice. But while democracy was the rule of the majority, it was also the rule of opinion as against knowledge. So better to mix the aristocratic principles of knowledge and skill (which on their own so easily degenerate, he said, into oligarchy, the rule of the powerful, or into plutocracy, the rule of the rich) with the democratic principles of consent and the power of numbers: 'the many electing the few'. (Not very 'democratic' in our sense, but a fair enough general description of what actually happens.)

And Aristotle's implicit assumption was that all forms of regime need to be justified, not merely philosophically, but also in practice, in order to ensure stability and survival. There is no such thing as 'naked power' without some rational consent, and what cannot be justified should be changed. The only justification for monarchy or rule by one person is that he or she is perfectly wise and perfectly good (which, in fact, Aristotle said would make that person a god – a theoretical possibility in Greek thought but unlikely in practice among professors, politicians, soldiers or civil servants). The only justification for aristocracy is wisdom and skill, but in practice pride and greed are more prominent. The only justification for democracy or the rule of numbers is equality (but the democratic justification on its own is to Aristotle a fallacy: 'the belief that because men are equal in some things they are equal in all'). So, better by far, he taught, to tie the skill of the few to the need to get the consent of the many – in short, to get the power of the people behind the state. Much of Roman political thought and practice was just a footnote to this basic point of political theory: '*auctoritas in Senatum, potestas in populum*' said Cicero ('authority in the Senate, power in the people').

Only in two important respects did the Romans add anything to the Greek heritage. They showed that some forms of republican institutions were possible on a very large territorial scale, whereas the Greeks had thought that both justice and stability were only possible in relatively small 'face-to-face' societies. Citizens could know each other well and thus settle divisive issues by discussion without constant recourse to the enforcement of laws. The very idea of 'empire', that is the rule of one culture over different cultures, seemed to the Greeks barbarous. But Roman law developed to embrace and mediate between, but not destroy, the laws of the conquered nations. Attempts were made to codify a higher law in the light of reason not just of custom. Also, Roman experience proved that citizenship need not be ethnic, based on common descent, as even the Greeks had believed, but rather based on rational allegiance to the spirit and laws of a state. Rome developed an explicit civic ideology which a stranger might learn, prove worthy of and adopt.

Both Greek and Roman culture attached supreme importance to the political. A man was himself at his best when he was acting as a citizen. To be a citizen you needed a mixture of knowledge, skill and courage. The Greeks called it *arete* and the Romans *virtu* – we don't have one word for it. This ideal image of man as participant citizen was never forgotten in the books of the learned, even though it did not recur in practice after the end of the Roman Republic until the Dutch Republic, and, the English, American and French Revolutions.

Of course, the legacy is more complicated than that. The economic liberalism that also arose in the era of revolutions was as much concerned to protect the new middle classes from politics as it was to open up political institutions to popular influence. Some liberals saw the dangers of democracy – what Alexis de Tocqueville famously called 'the danger of the tyranny of the majority'. They drew a sharp distinction between 'liberty' and 'democracy', contrary to the older republican tradition. Liberals concentrated on putting legal and constitutional restraints on state power, against both the monarch and the masses. Philosophically they tried to draw clear lines between minimum functions that the state must perform in the public realm and what it must never do by way of intruding on private life and property. But the older republican tradition of popular liberties and popular power never died out, and even the most anti-democratic liberals had to play democratic politics in post-revolutionary society.

In Rome Cicero had repeated Aristotle's famous claim, that 'politics is the master science'. He did not mean, of course, that it explained all other sciences as bodies of knowledge, but that only good political judgement (a mixture of knowledge and skill) can give all other 'sciences', and indeed the interests of social groups as well, some acceptable priority in their competing claims on scarce resources. Economics can tell us the price of something in terms of what else we have to forgo to get it, but politics alone can create a framework in which the distribution of goods and resources is acceptable and just. Of course politics must 'interfere with the market', about which Mrs Thatcher, for instance, complains so much. But to argue that *as much freedom as possible* should be left to the market and that the state should have absolutely minimal functions, is itself a powerful political argument with great political consequences. It *is* a matter of 'as much freedom as possible' on both sides, a relative and political matter: a totally free market or total central control of an economy are probably both as logically impossible as they are morally undesirable. Politics is unavoidable, even by those who attack it. Modern market economists have yet to make a reasoned reply to old Aristotle.

In the medieval world less importance was attached to political life, that is the tradition of seeking to resolve disputes in a political way by public debate. Many aspects of Christianity were, indeed, hostile both to the Greek and Roman pride in man the maker and man the shaper of his destiny, and to their glorification of civic culture and preoccupation with the stability of cities. In the fourth century AD St Augustine explained the fall of Rome; he taught that only the city of God is eternal: all earthly cities are creatures of time, as doomed to decay and death as wretched man himself. But he had a kind of realism when he said that human cities were not based on justice and reason but on brutal self-interest: they hang together for the same reasons that bands of robbers hang together.

Christian morality was different from classical (or 'pagan', as Christians called it) morality. For Aristotle, to be truly a man one must have the capabilities of citizenship, namely leisure and reason. He believed that women and slaves could not be citizens by nature. But to the Christian all men and women were at least spiritually equal, equally worthy and equally capable of salvation. 'Blessed are the meek for they shall inherit the kingdom of heaven.' St Paul preached that there was no difference between Jew and Greek: we are 'all children of one father'. It was not a democratic doctrine, because 'the kingdom' was not of this world and in this world we should 'suffer the powers that be'; it is for God not man to punish the oppressor. The Church became an hierarchical institution not, despite some attempted deviations, a collegiate one. But the concept of equality of souls planted a secular seed that could enable Rousseau, centuries later, to argue that good government should not be based upon knowledge and experience (as Aristotle had taught), but on sincerity. There was a natural simplicity and morality to be found (with a little guidance) in *every* common man (and, as Tom Paine and Mary Wollstoncraft were soon to add, every common woman).

A distinction grew up between 'divine law', the product of specific interventions by God, such as the inspiring of the scriptures and the creation of bishops as a sacred order, and 'natural law' which, as part of God's general creation, is accessible through reason to all men, and binding on all men, not merely Christians. Disputes as to what was properly a matter of divine or natural law, and as to who should decide, Pope or Emperor, were endemic, endless and sometime physically violent as well as theological. But it was of lasting importance that as a theology Christianity is *dualistic*: it allows the coexistence with the spiritual (even if at a lower level of importance) of a secular sphere which contains reason, political life and natural science. Christ himself had said, albeit somewhat engimatically, 'Give Caesar the things that are Caesar's, and God the things that are God's.' The Christian Church never quite destroyed the autonomy of science and politics – as happened in some other religions and was briefly attempted in some modern political ideologies.

Now it may or may not be that there is anything beyond the secular world open to our senses. Such speculation is, strictly speaking, irrelevant to the political tradition. For there to be political knowledge at all one does not have to say, like an eighteenth-century sceptic, 'disbelieve', only to note that Christian theology has always allowed a sphere of spiritually irrelevant, purely secular considerations. And even within the Church there must be room for a rational discussion of how certain beliefs can be imposed upon society, or upheld in the face of society. Even religions have to practise compromises if their adherents are to carry on peaceably living with the unsaved or the damned, or even with themselves. And if part of a Church's belief is the moral obligation of charity, compassion and love of one's fellows, it can hardly avoid appearing (as at the moment) politically 'controversial'. Some think that the Bishop of Durham, for instance, goes 'too far' in talking of political issues and social problems, others say 'not far enough'.

Machiavelli never really denied (though there is a very common belief that he did) conventional, that is to him, Christian, ideas of good and evil. On the contrary, he says quite clearly that in order to preserve the state it is sometimes necessary to do evil. Never, like Hegel, does Machiavelli say that all actions to further the survival of the state are necessarily good actions. He makes us aware, once again, of one of the most basic dilemmas of morals and politics: the agony of doing a bad action for a good cause, or the more subtle agony (experienced by so many in Eastern Europe) of trying to lead a decent, quiet and just life in an oppressive and corrupt regime. Nothing can guarantee that on some terrible occasions considerations of survival and considerations of morality do not conflict.

There are at least two good reasons why Machiavelli deserves to be honoured as the 'patron saint' of Politics: (i) he reminds us of the price to be paid for order and stability; and (ii) he attempted to study objectively the social conditions appropriate to different types of government.

He recognized, slightly amending Aristotle, that there were two basic forms of government, which he called 'princely rule' and 'republican rule'. The republic, like Aristotle's best possible *polis*, was a mixture of aristocracy and democracy, neither of which on its own, he believed, could ever prove stable. So Machiavelli in his *Discourses* set out to answer two essentially practical questions: (i) what circumstances are most fitting for either princely or republican rule? (ii) what is the best mixture of elements for long-term stability of the state?

His general theory was that republics cannot be established where there is no prior tradition, memory or practice of individual citizenship; and that where there is such a tradition, then a *principate* (we would say, a personal autocracy) can only be established by extraordinary violence, cruelty and skill. So, in general, principalities are inherently unstable. The way to create a new state, to reform a corrupt one or to save a republic from attack is by the leadership of an heroic individual. In order to preserve a state over time however, power must be shared and the state made over into a civic republic (as perhaps Mr Gorbachev is discovering). Machiavelli makes a dynamic analysis out of the somewhat static concepts of Aristotle. How useless, he thinks, is a state which cannot trust its own people with arms: the Roman Republic was strong because the Senatorial class had learned to ride, as it were, the tumult of popular politics, because allowing the common people to have representatives, called tribunes, meant that they felt part of the state themselves, which in war added vastly to its strength. 'SPQR' (the Senate and the people of Rome) was on the banners of the Roman legions. The people and the Senate fought together. Most autocracies have spent a lot of effort keeping arms out of the hands of their loving people.

Perhaps these ideas sound tied to a pre-industrial and pre-nuclear age of relatively simple military technology. But in the 1930s an Italian Marxist, Gramsci, argued that Machiavelli's theory holds up well in the modern world if one substitutes for the citizen soldier of his times the citizen worker of ours – that new key creature of the Industrial Revolution, the skilled industrial worker. It is on the willingness of the skilled worker to adapt and to work that the stability of modern states depends. He can only be ignored or suppressed at the price of industrial stagnation. The Soviets attempted to control him, at the price of creating a huge apparatus of propaganda, control, repression and inefficiency. For it now seems obvious in Eastern Europe and in the Soviet Union itself that such a system, although it can repress free speech, cannot prevent a most potent form of opposition or silent dissent – sullen apathy, indifference to working hard and working well and, when strikes are forbidden, even a sardonic satisfaction in working badly. One can see that in poorly paid workers everywhere.

I have risked boring you with a short history lesson because it is so important for both the study and practice of present-day politics to grasp the perennial nature of the political process, and to realize that it has not changed as much as we often assume. Some writers accept without question that the Industrial Revolution and the coming of capitalism have rendered these old categories of types of government as used by Aristotle and Machiavelli irrelevant or meaningless. Every year some social scientist invents a completely new vocabulary to describe the relationships between politics and society; but somehow they never catch on (beyond their own students) and we make do with the old terms. Liberal economists have argued that the best kind of state is a minimal state (one simply concerned with defence and law and order): a free market can make all essential decisions for us about the best distribution of resources, wages and rewards; and therefore the intrusion of 'political factors' can only spoil economic rationality. Marxists have also argued that political factors intrude, but to them they intrude by attempting to delay the consequences of economic laws which first heighten class conflict and then simplify the social structure into working-class dominance (the fancy word is 'hegemony'), and, ultimately, into a classless society. Marx himself said that politics is what the bourgeoisie do with their leisure, which is itself a product of exploitation, to try to maintain their class rule.

Hannah Arendt in her great book *The Human Condition* (Chicago, 1958) argued that the concepts of the Marxists and the liberal economists are just two sides of the same coin. They both object in different ways to politics intruding into economics. To each of them economics is the master science. But of course politics intrudes. The real world is like that. On our analysis politics and economics are complementary. Economics quantifies a sense of reality, but through politics we must gain *some* control over the market and enforce bargains between different views of 'what should be done?' The Thatcher governments have shown how much politics it takes to try to create and sustain an apparently politics-free market system! In fact there is no such thing. Ultimately any distribution of resources in society must be a political compromise.

There is no one overriding principle of organization which suits all peoples in all times and circumstances. That *should* be obvious. For instance, if we allow belief in 'free enterprise' or 'national sovereignty' to imply uncontrolled exploitation of natural resources, then we may be destroying the whole way of life of a region or nation or the fertility of the planet Earth itself. Similarly to believe 'my party right or wrong' is always potentially destructive of the rights, sometimes even the lives, of others. Orwell once said that 'a writer cannot be a *loyal* member of a political party'. He was himself a member of a political party when he wrote that.

We can all survive and do ourselves and our natural habitat less harm by accepting that there is, in fact, a plurality of moral ends in the real world. The student of politics should not ask people to accept that all ends are equally good – that would be nonsense: but while he or she is thinking politically, the argument must be that all moral ends must be understood, their inwardness grasped and tolerated, if only intellectually, even when disapproved of. Nothing can be taken out of politics that other people in a democracy want to make a political issue: not property, not religion, not 'law and order', not race relations even. We can only act prudently and use good or bad political judgement about *degrees* of control.

So political knowledge is very relevant. If we are to contain conflicts we must understand the motivations of the combatants (History and Psychology) and the social conditions in which they flourish (Economics and Sociology). If, on the contrary, we don't think politically of containment and compromise but only of 'victory for the true cause!', then we need no empathy or understanding of other viewpoints, or if so, only for tactical reasons; we only need, like desperate revolutionaries or bad generals, force, courage, luck and loyal (or stupid) followers. Understanding the motivations of others needs knowledge and imagination. Such understanding, or dispassionate political judgement, is actually a general condition for toleration and peace. Good political judgement not only helps compromise and control but also inhibits extreme solutions, making them seem risky and uncertain.

Political judgement is also an internal restraint. Most modern autocracies find it easier not to be arbitrary even if they are harsh and oppressive. Their inhabitants can discover, broadly speaking, what is legal and what is not legal; so they can at least keep out of trouble even if they have no freedom or influence. Even the worst governments find it prudent, broadly speaking, to stick to rules they have inherited or made themselves. But modern autocracies still have to conceal the reasons why decisions are made. They conceal them simply because they are made in the interests of particular groups, commonly the governing party, and not in the general interest. The 'general interest' can only mean anything when there is a general, open and reasonably free canvassing of opinions. *The very mark of a free society is not merely high rates of actual participation by ordinary citizens but is a public knowledge of why decisions are made.*

Participation could only be relevant and intense for all citizens in states the size of the Greek cities. But communications can be open, free and reasonably accurate in states of any size, thanks to radio and television. It is small wonder there is such sensitivity whenever governments in democracies try to control or threaten the media. The problems of sifting and digesting information are in practice formidable, but in principle purely technical.

Thus knowledge of politics, which itself can only flourish in relatively free societies, suggests that in the long run it is more difficult to govern large and complex societies in an autocratic rather than in a political manner. While it is most interesting and important to study autocracies and not underestimate their staying power, yet there is a built-in bias towards freedom in the very activity of studying politics, as in the concept itself.

This 'bias' in favour of politics itself and of studying how to resolve conflicts politically, rises above the actual political doctrines with which we are all most familiar, or rather it subsumes them. In one sense, for instance, the European political tradition can be seen as *conservative*. It leads us to see the continuities between social systems, to see that tradition is usually more influential than ideology (we do more things out of habit and by analogy than by conscious reason) and that *order* is needed for any kind of civilized life. The real conservative is less opposed to revolution than he (or she) is sceptical about claims to be able to transform 'this sorry scheme of things entire'. He suspects that Soviet foreign policy, for instance, showed a great deal of continuity with Tsarist policy – for both are products of common circumstances as well as of different intentions. And the real conservative fears anarchy more than that revolutionaries can really succeed in establishing a new and ideal order.

But in another sense the political tradition is perpetually *radical*. The Greeks thought that mankind could control their own fate and destiny by living together in civic communities. The political tradition, in this sense, becomes linked to the idea of conscious social change, breaking from ancient beliefs in a fixed order of things and static societies reflecting what the Manchu emperors called 'the mandate of heaven'. Most of us see no secular reason why we should 'suffer the powers that be' or accept that 'the poor are with you always'. We can study the *how* and the *why* of social change. We may not be able to make the world perfect but we can hope to make it better if we try hard, skilfully, patiently.

4

The politics of modern representative government

Economists and sociologists tend to assume that the institutions and thinking of the modern world are unique. But students of politics should be cautious. True, we now have many more classificatory schemes of types of government than can be found in Aristotle or Machiavelli's thought. But they arise far more from the very number of political scientists, from professional arguments about how best to describe the same old things in a more sophisticated way, than from new inventions of forms or devices of government. The modern world of politics has seen far fewer inventions than in science, technology and warfare. It is no accident that we tend to use much the same vocabulary as of old: autocracy, despotism, tyranny, democracy, republics, freedom and representation etc. These terms gain new meanings but without losing the old. New growths retain deep roots.

Perhaps there are only two great inventions of government in modern times: the practice of *party government*, both one-party rule and competitive party systems; and the practice of *totalitarian government*. Two regimes and two only emerged in the 1930s, Nazism and Stalinist Communism, which shared an aspiration towards a total control of society and possessed (or rather claimed to possess) an ideology which claimed to explain and give meaning to *everything* in society. To the totalitarian mind everything is politically relevant, art as much as economics; and all values are public values, none are private; there is no neutrality or permissable isolation. Carl Friedrich and Zbigniew Brzezinski in their *Totalitarian Dictatorship and Autocracy* (Harvard, 1956) produced a model which claimed six unique operating characteristics: an official and comprehensive ideology, a single mass party with a leader, a system of terror, a monopoly of communications, a monopoly of arms and total central control of the economy.

The debate has been fierce and complicated about whether such governments ever, even for a decade or two, really existed in such a form; or, even if they did, whether they are unique to the modern world. To some 'totalitarianism' is simply a category of aspiration (or abuse). Some have said, indeed, that the term is just anti-Communist propaganda, a product of the Cold War. There is at least broad agreement that some autocracies in the modern world have tried to be qualitatively different from old autocracies. Old autocracies favoured illiteracy among the masses; new autocracies promote literacy both for industrialization and for indoctrination. Old autocracies thrived on passive obedience and on letting sleeping dogs lie, whereas new autocracies try to mobilize all their inhabitants and to enforce the same belief-system on them all. But there is even more agreement that these attempts have failed (as Mr Gorbachev seems to realize).

Nazis and Communists both saw the parliamentary regimes as perpetuating problems rather than solving them and denounced representative government as hopelessly inefficient and historically doomed. But in the modern world, for all its terrible problems – perennial ones like poverty, disease and misgovernment, and new ones like the control of nuclear power and environmental despoilation – representative institutions have survived and flourished. Even regimes that are plainly not democratic usually claim to be. The old ideas of free government still seem to set the standard. Some parliamentary regimes have become military dictatorships, as in South and Central America; but as many have returned to free institutions. In Europe in the last 20 years, Portugal, Greece and Spain have each passed from military dictatorships into parliamentary regimes. Optimism is not in fashion, but pessimism is often exaggerated.

So a reasonable stability of government can be achieved amid high rates of social and technological change, not by new inventions but by adapting old devices and principles to new conditions. Parliaments adapt their procedures to support as well as to restrain governments. The parliamentary system of government is stable when strong government and strong opposition can coexist. Governments must govern, but they govern best if subject to the kind of criticism and scrutiny that parliaments can provide and focus – focus even when the impulses come from others: pressure groups, the press, the universities etc. Social theory should see modern parliaments neither as governments nor as representing 'the will of the people', but as two-way communication systems linking the two.

Freedom depends on the right to criticize governments, the ability to do so and on *citizens actually doing so*. 'Negative liberty' (that is liberty *from* the state) needs exercising positively. Even Lincoln's great aphorism is too weak: 'the price of liberty is eternal vigilance'. The price is even higher, surely, that of eternal activity. And freedom can work through many more institutions than parliament. A good A-Level question was once: ' *"Extra-parliamentary is not necessarily anti-parliamentary." Explain and discuss.*' At college you'll spend a lot of time discussing how far democracy should be and can be applied to many different types of social groups and institutions. None of them could work without parliament, although no modern British parliament can claim, like an eighteenth-century one, to have a monopoly on political activity.

It is not crucial to freedom that governments can be regularly defeated in parliament, but that they have to be re-elected periodically and can then be defeated. Competitive general elections are at least as important as parliamentary votes. Both need publicity. Governments are restrained as much by knowing that the press knows, or could know, why they make decisions, as they are by formal votes. Governments fear public opinion as it begins to crystalize in the form of voting intentions in the opinion polls. Parliaments can influence public opinion far more effectively than they can ordinarily influence government legislation.

Parliaments are then a vital part, a necessary but not a sufficient part, of republican or representative government. Following the failures of some parliaments in the 1930s and given the absence of any parliamentary institutions at all in most countries of the world, we must not claim too much. If government as basic law and order breaks down, no parliament can survive for long. Rather than speak of 'parliamentary government', it could be more accurate to say (with Professor S.E. Finer) 'government through parliament'. For the heart of the matter is the great difference between a government which has to argue its way through the publicized debates of a public assembly, and one that can keep its reasons and intentions to itself.

Parliaments do not simply represent popular opinion but also, as Professor Samuel Beer has argued in his *Modern British Politics* (1965), have to 'mobilize consent'. Democracies must do this quite as much as autocracies. The old story was a good one: a man in Paris in 1789 was talking to his neighbour when a crowd rushed by: 'Excuse me, I must go and catch them up, I'm their leader.' And there are aspects of specifically modern life about which governments can legislate until they are blue in the face but little will happen unless people change their behaviour: wage restraint, industrial relations, employment of women, community relations, alchohol and drug abuse and road safety are obvious examples. People persuaded are more effective than persons commanded. And parliaments can serve an early warning to governments if persuasion is likely to fail. Perhaps then the legislation will be withdrawn or amended.

Walter Bagehot in his famous essay *The English Constitution* argued that the importance of parliament lay less in its *legislative* function than in its *expressive, teaching* and *informing* functions. Even granted his antidemocratic bias (the book was not a monograph but a polemic in the Second Reform Bill controversy of 1867), few commentators now see parliament other than through Bagehot's eyes as (to update his language) a two-way communication system. The old Tory theory was that parliament was there to support the Crown's ministers, and the Radicals' theory saw it as the voice of the people (those people, at least, who were allowed to vote). They are both, in Bagehot's eyes, half-wrong and half-right: parliament mediates power and consent, the continuity of the state and changing democratic representation. (Lectures and books on parliament should be less dull and thoughtless than they commonly are: it is the heart of political life not just a traditional institution.)

Bagehot was the first to identify the importance of the cabinet in British government. But equally famously he missed the party, or rather only after the 1867 did it become clear that modern government was party government. Only then did disciplined party machines emerge outside parliament in the country, partly to support, partly to try to constrain, the older and looser, more personal and less ideological, aristocratic groupings of parliament. Parties still form the essence in all parliamentary regimes, providing coherence and consistency in policy and procedure. But some observers think that they now count for *relatively* less than they did even a generation ago. If you want to campaign for a cause, would you join a party or a pressure group?

Pressure groups have a great influence on policy, as often working on Whitehall's civil servants as on parties or on parliament. MPs often represent pressure groups, and gain special attention because of it. An MP is not ignored because, for instance, he is paid a retainer by the Police Federation to look after their interests; he is more likely because of that to catch the Speaker's eye in debates on law and order. Lobbying and interest group representation is now less secretive (more studied even), and generally the better for it.

Keith Middlemas argued in his *Politics in an Industrial Society* (1980) that between 1916 and 1979 Britain was a 'tripartite' system: the power of the state was a product not of the electoral system but of informal bargaining between 'the government machine', the City and industry, and the unions. It was Bagehot who first taught us to look beyond the 'dignified' façade into the real function of institutions.

In most modern states new networks of representative institutions are emerging, including trade unions but by no means limited to them (as was once thought would be the case), which probably strengthen representative government overall but leave the traditional parliament less important than it was. Parliaments, assemblies and congresses can now be seen as the *predominant* representative institution but no longer the *omnipotent* or sovereign one. Indeed we now tend to talk about 'government in a pluralistic society' rather than, as the old books did, about 'state and society'. 'Society' often used to imply the idea of a mass society, or even, it was rashly said, a relatively simple, homogenous social structure. Few messages from the centre sound the same when received in the different regions, the different cultures and even different nations in the United Kingdom. And therefore it is less easy, for better or worse, to stir the masses, to have a similar and predictable effect on everyone by one set of actions in the centre.

Even modern autocracies find the going harder. In the Third World as many dictators fall as rise, though the commonest problem is chronic instability rather than perpetual iron regimes. Many of the African military dictatorships or one-party states are, if oppressive, terribly weak regimes in the sense of being unable to carry out 'premeditated intentions', to keep the peace and stimulate the economy. Eastern Europe has several unchallengeably powerful governments who are powerless to stimulate the economy, though excellent at enforcing order. Even the Soviet Union itself now begins to show signs of realizing that propaganda for the masses without results for the consumer is an inefficient way to run an economy. There is no love of liberty there, only a new and welcome political realism in Gorbachev's policy of *glasnost*.

More and more it is recognized that the kind of economic and social policies needed in modern society cannot be enforced by command but have to be persuasive, convincing and responsive to the opinions of both managers and skilled workers. And modernization depends upon positive responses in the everyday behaviour of ordinary people. Political and industrial relations, even in the most democratic regimes, are often a product of what people will put up with or accept rather than what they positively agree with or actively want. But there are limits to what a skilled worker will put up with. Rebellion is not always the ultimate or indeed possible sanction against an autocratic government: more effective may simply be working reluctantly, slowly, indifferently, badly. Much of Eastern Europe represents a vast, informal and quite unplanned 'go slow' movement, severely limiting the powers of government.

Some see threats to freedom in the dependence of modernizing governments on technologists and experts whose culture is not political, in the conventional sense of experiencing and enjoying open-ended debate and speculation. Defence experts tend to be like that. They live in a world in which there is a correct answer to every precise problem, not in one of bargaining and compromise. But extreme dependence on them only comes if politicians and civil servants are ignorant of science and technology. The existence of 'two cultures' mutually incomprehensible and hostile is indeed as dangerous as similar divisions of social class. The only long-term answer is educational reform, but middle-term solutions involve more effective popularization of both scientific problems and political issues. The interaction between science and politics can be seen by studying such episodes as the debate about the causes and remedies of the Ethiopian famine of 1985–6; the advantages and disadvantages of nuclear power; and, most recently, public policy on the Aids epidemic.

To end as we began. There is a lot to be said for the continuing relevance of the first general theory of politics. Aristotle put forward two criteria for stability in the *polis*. The first is famous: that men should rule and be ruled in turn (and he did not mean alternation of professional political leaders but that a broad class of citizens should take turns in office, rather like a jury system). The second is now forgotten and sounds bizarre: that the state should be no larger than that a *Stentor* (someone with a legendary loud voice) could be heard from one side to the other; or, he put the same point another way, no larger than one in which citizens could know each other's character and therefore act justly, not just apply general rules impersonally. Traditionally this was thought to limit democracy, as Rousseau believed, to small groups; and therefore democracy was often rejected.

The modern *Stentor*, however, can be the press, radio and television. Tens of millions can hear the government spokesmen, the opposition and even listen to themselves in phone-ins, panel programmes and interviews. Through all this we can 'know each other's character' – if not that of individuals, certainly of other groups. Half the time half of us are watching how the other half live. The media should prevent things going to extremes and create some knowledge of other groups in our own society, even if its intention is often only to entertain. Orwell in *Nineteen Eighty-Four* rudely satirized the popular press as offering only 'prolefeed' – sex, violence and sport – to divert people's minds from real issues. The press is a force both for good and for ill.

All this may have seemed very abstract but it is vital to be clear about the starting point. It is meaningless to describe the divisions of an academic discipline without characterizing the general nature of the problems it studies. Study problems not subjects, as the philosopher Karl Popper has taught! We go wrong at the beginning, less often at the end. It is the basic concepts which are difficult, often because they seem so simple, being used in so many different ways in everyday speech. Any trained monkey with a Ph.D. can elaborate complicated variations of other people's ideas on a computer. The assumptions of the discipline have to be exposed. Most courses just plunge in. But the student must always put to Politics the political questions: why is the subject taught this way rather than that? What alternatives are there to the views so confidently (and often) put forward?

Social scientists are very apt to claim either scientific status or a professional neutrality. We should be objective about evidence. But the discipline is no more purely scientific than is medicine: diagnosis is also an art. Just as medicine's whole object is health, the care and prevention of disorders and diseases, so the whole presupposition and object of Politics is freedom and representative government. We have to be quite as interested in pathology and disease as doctors. We don't spend our time admiring healthy bodies, admirable though they are; we too are peculiarly interested in disorders. Our advice is not always worth much and is seldom taken by governments, but that is a different matter. None the less we do have general theories that point (other things being equal) to the superiority of representative institutions over permanent autocracies.

You will find that most political scientists who would think that this sounds very political or 'ethnocentrically liberal' and who try to avoid value judgements and study politics as scientifically and therefore as statistically as they can, none the less study mainly the politics of representative institutions. This is partly because the evidence that they need to play their role of being scientists is much more readily available and reliable in parliamentary regimes, and partly because they are simply deceiving themselves. We should be objective (our favoured regime or party may be mortally ill, and we, unlike the politicians, have to say so openly), but we cannot be neutral. Liberty is a precondition of the advancment of learning. In some societies the pursuit of learning is infinitely harder than in others, political learning especially.

Freedom is a matter of social relationships, of interactions, not simply of the assertion of individual personality:

anarchists mislead as much as economic liberals. It is simply not true that we always pursue our naked self-interest. Your self and my self are as we are not just by our individual will but because of how other people see us and behave towards us, which is affected by how we see them and behave towards them, and they to each other. All social interaction involves voluntary restraints. Political freedom means interaction with other citizens and each accepting the equal rights of others.

If we want to live freely ourselves and value freedom for others, whether we are élitist or egalitarian, what alternatives are there to parliaments or assemblies? The only alternatives on offer in the modern world are one-party rule or military government. No one has seriously argued for rule by a scientific élite since the death of H.G. Wells. That argument today is only found in science fiction and fantasy literature.

Machiavelli gives good arguments in *The Prince* why a concentration of power is necessary to create or restore a state; but he was equally clear in *The Discourses* why it is then prudent and good for power to be spread, for republican institutions to be adopted, if the state is to survive through time.

Surely the wise theorist, like the shrewd activist, should be willing patiently to distinguish different levels and time-scales of theory? The prospect of inter-party democracy in the Soviet Union, for instance, at least opens the door to the distant possibility of democracy between different parties. The prospect is not to be condemned as 'undemocratic' (or 'unAmerican' or whatever) because it falls short of ideal standards, or is not likely to happen tomorrow. Surely different time-scales are appropriate to different circumstances? Rome wasn't built in a day. If there is, for instance, to be 'reconciliation of the two communities' in Northern Ireland, or, even more ambitiously, 'unity with consent', then we are talking objectively of at least a generation. A fundamental change of social attitudes would be involved; and from all we know in history and the social sciences that must mean, even if the political will is there, that a new generation has to come up through the schools with teachers who share the new aspirations, while the old misleaders die out.

The form of representative institutions and the ideas associated with them will vary with every different culture.

Attempts to impose ready-made institutions from one society on to another usually fail, or rather have quite unexpected and often unwelcome results. Political Sociology and Comparative Government study these 'fits' and 'misfits'. And most of us don't think in terms of causal laws but rather of conditioning factors. 'What was the cause of the French Revolution?' is either a bad or a trick question; the answer must always be: 'there were several main conditions . . . and possibly their relative importance was. . . .' Not believing that there is ever a single explanation or cause for a social event is itself part of political freedom. Political science is not value-free. It is committed to freedom. The student of politics should not be value-free, but that is no licence to commit oneself to a cause if it is at the cost of professional integrity: we are committed to freedom, to truth, to objectivity and to relevance.

5

Types of political thought

Ideas and objectivity

The distinction in syllabuses between 'ideas' and 'institutions' is highly conventional. A social institution, whether family, firm, party or parliament, is an embodiment of ideas and purposes. And all ideas seek some lasting institutional form, whether in law, churches, parties, pressure groups or nations. Anthropologists, for instance, frequently speak of concepts as institutions, like honour, shame, revenge, compassion, friendship etc. Some have said that to understand the typical concepts of a society is to understand that society. Ernest Gellner put it better: 'to understand the *working* of its concepts is to understand a society'. None the less, some people are very conventional (always studying the one or the other, 'ideas' or else 'institutions'), and most syllabuses are constructed that way. Again, to follow Gellner, most moral ideas are conventional but there have to be conventions, there have to be syllabuses.

Take clothes. They are necessary, especially in cold climates. But all fashions are arbitrary. We may not be up on the latest nor want to be, but then almost certainly we are following some old fashion or convention. But most of us don't take the question of what to wear too seriously, far less seriously than being sure of having something to wear at all. We mainly wear what we do wear in this world of restless change with a kind of ironic detachment or temporary affection. So too with political ideas. We may when young try on several different sets for size, so long as they don't take us over completely.

In the social sciences ideas take on a more systematic form as theories. The theories of social scientists are necessarily concerned with three levels of inquiry: *What is the case?, what is thought to be the case?* and *what ought to be the case?* There are some purists in political philosophy, in Britain mainly connected with the school of Professor Michael Oakeshott, who deny that the third level has any place in the study of the discipline. But most of us think that to be an elaborate form of self-deception, at the least. There are also some self-styled political scientists (sometimes called, as we will see, 'behaviourists') who share the same view for quite different reasons, believing in a fully *scientific* study, and to whom the same remark applies. This logical trinity applies to the study of institutions and the study of thought alike. If someone studies, for instance, how the cabinet works, the first two dimensions are obvious but it would seem extraordinary if they had no views on what it should be doing and how it might work better. Indeed to understand the significance of the resulting work we would need to form some idea of the general viewpoint of the author, what can be discounted, what he or she takes for granted.

Sometimes people try to get around this difficulty by adherence to 'the doctrine of the two hats'. They say: 'as a political scientist I observe that . . .' and, 'as a citizen I think this . . .'. 'I've built the neutron bomb, now let's discuss whether it should ever be used or not.' (This can become almost split-minded.) I am not saying that one should not strive to be objective in any account of how an institution works or when deciding what meaning to attach to a political document, ancient or modern. One should and one can succeed, if one is knowledgeable, empathetic and honest. The only ultimate test will be, as in all science, whether someone else can independently repeat much the same work and come up with much the same conclusion. But each result will, if recognizably similar, have a different shading or colouring.

Yet not having the courage to tell the truth can have disastrous consequences. In 1946 both Russian and American civil servants told their masters what they wanted to hear. In the one case their lives and in the other their jobs depended on it. So they reported that 'the American working class' was on the edge of revolt, and that 'support for the Chinese Communist party among the common people' was crumbling. They may have bought time for themselves but there were grave practical consequences for policy-making on the basis of false information. A regime that is able to get even 'the inner party' to testify that two plus two equals five may be demonstrating their immediate power; but in the long run they are in for bad trouble.

'Know thy enemy as thyself', Arthur Koestler once said to George Orwell. Those two men as writers and journalists had an almost perverse integrity and objectivity in telling their own side what it did not want to hear. We should have that integrity as students of politics at all times. We cannot but be critics as well as observers. The drama critic for the local newspaper who tries not to be critical, only purely descriptive, ends up condoning rubbish and (if anyone believed him) misleading people. A totally objective BBC would get like that. But we must not deceive ourselves that because we are students and scholars we do not have prejudices and values ourselves. The more we are aware of them, the *more* objective we can be. Both self-examination and being objective can be psychologically and morally quite painful. If you are in favour, for instance, of the dismantling of nuclear power stations, do you automatically believe that supplies of coal and oil will be enough to maintain industrial civilization into the mid-twenty-first century? The political debate cannot be rational unless based on difficult but genuine interpretations of scientific evidence – not just the intoning of mere words like 'we *can* develop alternative technologies!' Perhaps, but perhaps not. A less dramatic example is the prediction of general election results. If the pollster has views he must not let them interfere with the technical accuracy of the research. He is restrained, just as if engaged in conventional scholarly activity, by personal honesty, professional ethics and by competition – other pollsters and other scholars can cover the same ground. No wonder scholars are suspicious of books by journalists who either 'cannot reveal' their sources or 'do not wish to weary the reader with an elaborate apparatus of scholarly footnotes'. As I write I am thinking that a coming general election result is probable that I do not entirely welcome.

By the time you read this, that last sentence may mean something entirely different to what I now intend it to convey. You will need to date it and put it into context to establish its meaning. You are into the study of political thought, you are not just looking at a text but at the presuppositions behind it and at its context.

Political opinion, theory and doctrine

A cluster of important words and concepts get used somewhat promiscuously: political 'thought', 'theory', 'philosophy', 'ideas' and 'opinion'. These are all in usage, and one cannot make (or hope to enforce) laws about language; nor do authoritative definitions settle problems – at best, they may be useful. But we need to try to speak consistently if we are to be understood. There are different modes of political thinking which are sometimes confusingly described by a confusion of several of these names. I want to suggest a usage that will describe what goes on in the discipline even if it will be tighter than most people use (and others may use one of the other names to mean much the same thing). Some people talk about the 'History of Political Ideas', some the 'History of Political Thought', and others (somewhat misleadingly, I think) put down 'Political Philosophy' in the syllabus when you may find that in fact it is not philosophizing, but an attempt at a purely descriptive history of political thinkers.

By *political opinion* is meant the ordinary opinions that people hold, their immediate demands, assumptions and reflections about public affairs. I mean something broader than 'public opinion' in the sense of popular attitudes to issues or policies, something that Bagehot called 'the political conversation of mankind'. Popular discourse is not just reactive to the issues the ladies and gentlemen up there or those in the media put to them down here. It contains conceptions of values and principles and of how the political world works which, however vague, even contradictory, usually inadequate and often wrong, are not different in kind from the reflections of philosophers and social theorists. Too often political scientists have limited their studies of opinion to the measurement of popular attitudes to specified issues, especially those relevant to voting behaviour. The kind of work done by anthropologists and social anthropologists on the operative belief-systems of a whole society has rarely been attempted by political scientists, even on interesting sub-groups like party political activists. We either rely on direct observation, however occasional and spasmodic, or on over-structured questionnaires. None the less, we have opinions and we study opinions, and opinions are not just about this or that, they contain principles, values and general understandings.

Opinion may seek to explain, but not in any systematic, scientific or scholarly way – as when we say that someone is 'opinionated'. This means, firstly, that they seem to have very little evidence for what they are saying, or respect for evidence; and secondly a noticeable amount of inconsistency as they apply their familar opinions to very different cases, never having really 'sorted their ideas out', so firing off on this and that. So often the only consistency that can be found is a psychological not a philosophical one, revealing more about the person than that person can tell us about the real world.

Theory is the highest form of structured opinion. By a political theory I mean attempts to *explain* the attitudes and actions arising from ordinary political life. Such explanations will take the form of *generalizations* about the relationship between concepts and circumstances. A theory must have a consistent and coherent language of explanation, but it is more than something that is 'true by definition' or 'true if you grant these premises'; it must be true in relation to external evidence and observations repeatable by others – or at least be logically capable of being *refuted*.

So political theory, strictly speaking, is hard to distinguish from the best political sociology, and a good deal of the history of political thought is nowadays basically concerned with the social context in which concepts gain their meaning. Though, for instance, Politics as a discipline has never been allowed to develop properly at Cambridge, some of the best political sociology comes from sociological theorists there, and perhaps it is no accident that the most learned of contemporary British political philosophers, Professor Quentin Skinner, is there. His two-volume *The Foundations of Modern Political Thought* (Cambridge, 1979) looks beyond the texts of great political thinkers into the assumptions of the state papers and ordinary political writing of the day, trying to see how political concepts were actually used in early modern society.

So confused have terms become that at least two departments offer courses on 'Empirical Political Theory'. To my ears it sounds as odd as saying 'True British Government' or 'Real Public Administration'. But to their ears obviously 'Political Theory' has too often meant 'Political Philosophy', which at worst involves reading the texts of Plato, Hegel and Marx as if they were self-contained literary entities, or at best a purely linguistic, analytical approach to political concepts – 'what *can* freedom mean?' But the study of a concept should lead one to ask: 'what do people and politicians mean by it and what have they meant by it?' Theory must unite empirical observation and collection of evidence with the clarification of the meaning of ideas. Indeed even if you wanted simply to do *any* piece of empirical field work or desk-data analysis without considering whether it was politically or morally important (perhaps as a training exercise, or to test a methodology), if the terms used were not both tightly defined and also related to ordinary language and opinion, then the data gathered would be virtually meaningless and its interpretation arbitrary.

The best Comparative Government is also another way of looking at political theory. When cross-cultural comparisons are made, of how either institutions or ideas with the same names, with *something* in common, function in different societies, then not merely is this a kind of political theory, but it needs to draw on the whole body of traditional political theory – as well as a knowledge of the history of the countries concerned. Oddly, there have been very few attempts at histories of government in both a sociological *and* an historical mode. After all, the most usual explanation for why something is as it is, is that something analogous happened earlier.

So a political theory seeks to generalize and explain. A *political doctrine* is a systematic argument. But to be systematic, it must have some theoretical view of which social institutions are important and of what is the likely consequence if the recommended course of action is undertaken (or the grievous consequences if the course of action is not undertaken). Every doctrine presumes a theory. No one puts forward a political doctrine if they do not believe that in some circumstances, which they can specify, it will work. The sociologist Hobhouse put it very neatly: 'the ethically desirable must be the sociologically possible'. And nearly every theory, whatever the theorists themselves may think ('I'm only looking', 'I'm completely without bias', 'I'm only counting heads'), contains, assumes or conceals a doctrine. So a political doctrine is simply the active voice or the persuasive mood of theory.

The distinction between political theory and doctrine is not absolute, but it is important. It is *not* the business of a teacher of Politics, for instance, to 'take a stand', honestly announce his commitment and seek to persuade the eager or credulous young. (In my experience, more students switch off when they hear the rising whine of the preacher's voice than are moved to action, still less to thought.) I'll defend publicly anyone's right to their own political views if they are lucky enough to be attacked for airing them, but privately I'll often hint at self-indulgence and lack of professionalism. Professionalism is getting students, in the words of the late Harold Laski, 'both to think for themselves and to see the inwardness of other viewpoints' – something he himself notoriously found difficult! Indeed, I'm not so sure that he didn't actually say 'the inwardness of *the* other viewpoint' – a very fore-shortened universe.

Well, let's consider Laski's 'the other viewpoint' – conservatism presumably. It is undoubtably a doctrine. Until Mrs Thatcher and the liberal economist disciples of F.A. Hayek hijacked it, it preached the virtues of experience, established order, continuity, and even social hierarchy and the trusteeship of the traditional élite. We should be governed by people with long experience in government. We are happier when we know our place and role in society ('My Station and Its Duties' was a famous essay by a Victorian philosopher, F.H. Bradley); and happier too when we are not in a state of constant uncertainty, still less held down by the state, or up in an enforced social equality. Edmund Burke said 'We reform in order to preserve'. But his conservative doctrine is also a theory: it holds that the rise and fall of society is best explained in terms of the skill, will, knowledge and experience of a traditional élite (of which 'the English gentleman' was the ideal image); and also that most human behaviour arises from habit and tradition not from reason. Indeed it is a theory that can help explain a good many, though by no means all, historical circumstances.

The study of revolution, for instance, cannot simply assume that genuine revolutions have taken place, still less that they would have taken place had they not been 'betrayed'. The conservative historian may point coolly to formidable continuities between Tsarist and Stalinist Russia. Or like Tocqueville on the French Revolution, he will both theoretically and temperamentally focus on the reasons for the breakdown of the Old Regime, and waste few words on the revolutionary's claims that it collapsed because it was pushed or because he read the iron laws of historical development correctly. The socialist's question 'how far has the revolution fulfilled its aims?' will seem to a conservative almost a meaningless question. (This is not to say, of course, that the pre-revolutionary regime may not have fallen by the ineptness, ignorance and inflexibility of some traditionalist governments – it is much easier to be wise after the event.)

Socialist doctrine (to summarize brutally) argues for an egalitarian and fraternal society and looks to the future. Its theory claims that the rise and fall of societies is to be explained not by the adequacies or inadequacies of traditional élites, but in terms of the relationship of a new human type, the skilled industrial worker, to the control of the means of production. The doctrine of liberalism argues for independence, liberty and individualism, and the theory argues that the rise and fall of societies is to be explained by whether or not the market can be freed from all but a minimal and protective state control, and that the existence of the individual inventor and the self-made entrepreneur as cultural heroes is crucially important.

Political philosophy

Political philosophy is either analytical or substantive. Let me explain. It used nearly all to be substantive. From the time of Plato onwards people believed that there were direct correct answers to questions like: 'why should I obey the state?' (or, more often, 'are there circumstances in which I should not obey the state?'), 'what is justice?', 'how tolerant should we be of heresy and error?', 'what should be the limits of the power of the state?', 'how do we reconcile rights with duties?'. The 'correctness' of answers must either come from a religious and theological framework, which needs philosophy to mediate between it and secular and political life, or assumptions about the very nature of philosophy. The idealist theory of truth held that the use of moral terms demonstrates that there is a moral reality, not just ideas of justice relative to time and place and circumstances, but a true ideal of justice. In other words, it can be believed that there are higher criteria for philosophical judgements themselves, usually thought of as metaphysics.

Most modern philosophers do not think like that, especially in the Englisn and Scottish tradition that was first powerfully stated in the scepticism of David Hume. We cannot know such things. We can only know what is available to our senses and to our reason in the sense of logical consistency, not of metaphysical intuition. We cannot say what is morally true in any absolute sense, only what is meaningful. A great deal of political philosophy is not unlike a very complex and contentious Use of English paper. We cannot say what is *the* meaning of 'democracy', only what people have meant by it in different contexts. Nor can we say what *is* the true meaning of 'liberty', but only analyse how the term is used, how it could be used, whether a particular usage contradicts the use of other concepts in an argument, and what the consequences are of applying a particular usage or definition to a particular circumstance, moral or political problem. The role of philosophy is more often seen as *clarifying* arguments than *deciding* them; the political philosopher can sometimes eliminate a bad argument or a vague or self-contradictory definition, but he can never pontificate.

English philosophers are very fond of 'liberty', the concept – as in Sir Isaiah Berlin's famous inaugural lecture at Oxford, *Two Concepts of Liberty* (Oxford, 1958) and the vast critical literature that followed it. Some of us lament that most of this literature gets more and more inward-looking and technical. John Stuart Mill wrote his great essay *On Liberty* (with Harriette Taylor's help) to address a general if well-read public (though not by any means a university-educated one – a lot of people used to read important books without them being on a syllabus). Most political philosophy now is written by political philosophers for political philosophers. Its public role (which I tried to summarize in Chapters 3 and 4) seems all but lost. At least Berlin addressed himself to intellectuals, with only a minimum of disciplinary reference. Raymond Aron, the great French political theorist and political writer, although a

professor at the Sorbonne, used to claim that he wrote all his books for readers of *Le Monde*. One could wish that more political philosophers wrote as if for readers of the *Observer*, especially since there has been a remarkable revival of political philosophy in the last twenty years, both in Britain and in the United States. Most political philosophers, indeed, write with a clarity and directness which are not always found in the social sciences. The younger generation of political philosphers, moreover, apply the verbal, analytical logical technique more and more to real problems and real ethical dilemmas, rather than to hypothetical ones.

There is a sense in which political philosophers attempt to resolve intellectual conflicts when two or more political theories appear to give an equally plausible explanation of the same circumstances, as can easily happen. Some say they can only clarify such disputes, some say that there are ethical concepts, or general understandings of terms like 'rights', that can actually or should actually settle disputes wherever theories and doctrines clash. Certainly much modern political philosophy is interested in applying pure philosophy, of whatever type, not simply to political concepts, but also to political problems. It thus considers the kind of evidence that political sociologists produce about the mutual conditioning of ideas and circumstances.

History of political thought

Therefore the history of political thought (that is taught in all but the most 'scientifically-minded' departments) now tends to be much more concerned with sociological issues, the social setting of ideas, and more related to intellectual history and social history, than when once its only ally was the history of philosophy.

The good old staple product is still taught: a largely descriptive run through the history of political thought from Plato to the present, though sometimes the ride begins at a modern station called Machiavelli. It is not so much history, in the sense of contexts and interconnections and an attempt to recover the presuppositions of the past, as a chronological reading of famous texts by philosophers about political dilemmas in order to answer anachronistic modern questions.

But there are so many places to be visited that there is rarely much time left to discuss these questions. Sometimes the lecturer or the textbook (which often stands as substitute for the texts rather than as introducer) puts in some background. I am slightly parodying. However quick the journey it is important to have some rough idea of what some really great minds said both on the particular problems of their times and on some that have always struck readers, generation after generation, as perennial.

Such a course will, in the best practice, not be offered on its own as 'all the political thought you need', but as an introduction to one of two things, or a sensible combination of both. There can be the slow and close reading of a complex text – it hardly matters which (Aristotle, Hobbes, Hegel, Mill or Marx) so long as you have had such an experience; or the study of a special period of political thought in relation to the society and politics of its time. Again, though students often have fierce preferences for the modern period, it hardly matters which, for, whatever period you take, you learn a critical technique that can then be applied elsewhere, even to the reading of government or company reports. Best of all is when the two methods are combined. A text cannot simply be reduced to its context – as if Machiavelli was a *typical* Italian of his day who simply responded to the political problem of keeping his job and his head, or as if Hobbes was simply an early defender of the emerging capitalist economy (which emerged about twice a century since 1400 you'll discover). There were so many other Italians and Englishmen who didn't write profound books of genius. So combine both text and context: *read the text, then consider the context, then back to the text*.

Political Thought and Political Philosophy tend to dominate the subject intellectually at the London School of Economics (LSE) and at Oxford, with numerous options and specialists. They are the great powers beyond much doubt. But the standards are high almost everywhere, even where just one person holds the fort; and clusters of notable talent plainly occur elsewhere, for instance at Cambridge, Manchester, Lancaster, Glasgow, Hull, York, Swansea, Exeter, Durham, Southampton, Queen's Belfast and East Anglia.

History of political doctrines and movements

There are movements which may not produce great philosophy but are of real political importance and are dominated by ideas, or at least appear to be so. So there is a great deal of study of doctrines or of *ideologies* and the social or political movements associated with them. (I think of an ideology most simply as a comprehensive doctrine expressing the interests of some social group or class. But there is a vast literature on the concept and some strict Marxists would still hold that all ideas, including philosophical ideas, are merely ideology in the sense that they are a derivative expression of class interest or of rival modes of production.) The French and American Revolutions are often looked at as a study in ideologies, and so too the rise of the labour movement, socialism, populism and feminism etc.; and perhaps above all in its unexpected importance in the modern world, *nationalism* and its bastard cousins, racialism and fascism.

Some department syllabuses show signs of uncertainty about how best to fit all this in. Are movements ideas or institutions? Obviously they relate to both. Sometimes they figure in 'Comparative Politics' (especially if that term marks a deliberate distinction from 'Comparative Government'). Sometimes movements are seen as almost the whole matter of political theory as I have described it, generalizing and explaining, in contrast to philosophy analysing and judging. Sometimes this study is found better places in history or sociology departments or as joint papers or combined subjects. A few bold departments make it the very centre of their teaching, saying that if you concentrate on political and social movements you'll pick up a fair amount of knowledge about ideas and institutions along the way. Perhaps. One cannot do everything. The opinions of teachers and the demands of students vary. Sometimes it seems to be nowhere in particular but to permeate all the syllabus. This is a bit bewildering if you look at different syllabuses, but it is something to do with the liveliness of the subject and the open-ended nature of the activity itself.

There is a famous passage in Michael Oakeshott's introduction to the Blackwell edition of Hobbes's *Leviathan* (1946):

Reflection about political life may take place at a variety of levels. It may remain on the level of the determination of means, or it may strike out for the consideration of ends. Its inspiration may be directly practical, the modification of the arrangements of a political order in accordance with the perception of an immediate benefit; . . . or it may seek a generalisation of that experience in a doctrine. And reflection is apt to flow from one level to another, following the mood of the thinker. Political philosophy . . . [is] when this movement of reflection takes a certain direction and achieves a certain level, its characteristic being the relations of political life, and the values and purposes pertaining to it, to the entire conception of the world that belongs to a civilisation. . . . For any man who holds in his mind the conceptions of the natural world, of God, of human activity and human destiny that belong to this civilisation, will scarcely be able to prevent an endeavour to asssimilate these to the ideas that distinguish the political order in which he lives, and failing to do so he will become a philosopher (of a simple sort) unawares.

By 'failing', says Oakeshott, to assimilate our general ideas to those of our time, one becomes a philosopher. A strange thought, you may think, for a conservative, or for a democratic socialist like myself, to admire. But political philosophy deals in dilemmas because no practical solutions are ever fully successful, or last. And we never achieve exactly what we may plan to achieve; but that is no argument (as I suspect it would be for Oakeshott) for not trying to achieve anything radically new. 'All revolutions are failures', said Orwell (sounding pessimistic), 'but they are not all the same kind of failure' (which is actually a rather optimistic comment, the more you think about it). We cannot build lasting institutions because we cannot all agree, in every respect, what we are building for – which is (if one values freedom) probably as well.

6
Political institutions

Structures of government

'Political institutions represent attempts to define rules for conducting the business of politics which necessarily express those perceptions of political values which prevail at a given time in a society and especially in the minds of the politically active individuals within it.'* That is an excellent definition, it is worth brooding on and, as philosophers say, 'unpacking' slowly.

Any political institution, be it parliament, a party, a pressure group, or a type of election, is a set of rules, both formal and informal. Sometimes most of them are written down. There is a constitution, rule book or rules of order. Sometimes most of them are informal and are learned by being part of that institution and wanting, or needing, to observe its rules. I've never sat down to read through the constitution of my political party. The rules one ordinarily needs one picks up simply by being a member. The constitution is only consulted if there is a dispute about what the rules are. So institutions are 'attempts to define rules' which do not always succeed, either in encapsulating the actual rules observed by the politically active or in restraining aspects of their behaviour.

The metaphor of a game may help. In one sense, politics is *not* a game, for the consequences can be beneficial or even deadly for vast numbers of non-players. Yet it would be silly to deny that most politicians and political activists, while they have a sense of duty about how to play or practise politics, may

*Nevil Johnson, 'The Place of Institutions in the Study of Politics', in F.F. Ridley, ed., *Studies in Politics: Essays to mark the 25th anniversary of the Political Studies Association* (Oxford, Clarendon Press, 1975), p. 160.

none the less be motivated as much by enjoyment of the stern activity of struggle as by the sense of duty they present on the hustings or when answering the impertinent interviewer's question on the box.

However, it is *like* a game in that we learn the rules by playing it or watching it. The rules have no absolute authority: we obey them if we want to play that game; or we argue for their amendment in order to make it a more acceptable and enjoyable game – both to play and to watch. When I used to referee under-eleven football, the kids would sometimes bellow, 'You don't know the **** rules!' I'd mutter, 'Nor do you', and I'd shout, 'Play to the whistle!'. They did, for the good utilitarian reason that otherwise there would have been no game; they would have been in Hobbes's state of nature, anarchy: they needed a referee, however shaky his grasp of the rules, in order to play football at all. They had learned by playing with older boys and watching football, mainly on television. Only when their skills increased and we began to play other teams did I begin to ask and read about the offside rule, and occasionally to enforce it. It simply didn't make for a good game if two strikers lurked in the goal mouth all the time, but nor did it if I applied the rule too strictly.

A game is a purely traditional activity. Political institutions also arise from tradition. And they embody traditional values, those 'which prevail at a particular time in society'. Of course, as values change and as institutions through time encounter new problems (whether social or technological change, or external threats), they adjust and adapt. The late-twentieth-century House of Commons still has a very traditional atmosphere, and its proceedings are a strange mixture of rules and conventions (or better to say of written and unwritten rules); but it is a very different place from the late-nineteenth-century parliament. Both the modern Labour and the Conservative parties have made considerable deliberate changes in their constitutions, but these documents alone would be a poor guide to what they actually do.

Now, it is in the nature of institutions that they are not mechanical or electronic mechanisms that were designed at one time for a single clear purpose, and which can be scrapped, replaced or radically redesigned for wholly new purposes. If we changed the rules of cricket too completely there would be a point at which it would simply cease to be cricket. When parliament is reformed neither the intentions nor the expectations of reformers are completely fulfilled, because of tradition, because institutions are creatures of time, that is historical not biological or mechanical entities: many of the players carry on in much the same old way, though under a new, or partly new, set of rules and limitations.

It could be argued that institutions are inherently conservative. They always frustrate premeditated rational intentions. This was maintained by philosophical anarchists and by a peculiar school of socialists in the 1960s, of whom Herbert Marcuse was the most famous, who made a slogan of 'deinstitutionalization'! An educational reformer, Ivan Illich, put an interesting case for 'deschooling'. But it became progressively clear that their projects were literally impossible: they were only aiming to substitute the old institutions they disliked with some new institutions they favoured. In Illich's scheme home-learning and computer-linked public libraries and resource-banks were to replace compulsory school – which would require very elaborate organization both for provision and use. No kind of institution can avoid rules. Just as football players may not know the rules, and still play well, so anarchists in a commune may think they have no rules. But in each case a sensitive observer would be able to infer their actual rules from their behaviour. Highly charged personalities simply cannot live together without conventions. And even when a party or (as past ages used to dream) a good king or a benevolent despot give a society 'new institutions for a new age', it is extremely unlikely that the working of the new rules would not be affected by habit, analogy and custom.

The difficulty is not solved by a written constitution. For no constitution can possibly be either totally unambiguous or totally prescient of what new problems could occur in the future, unthought of by the Founding Fathers. In all institutions conventions grow up about the interpretation and reinterpretation of the basic rules. None the less, if we cannot escape the past entirely, institutions are for our use and we can and should change and adapt them both in light of new circumstances and changing values.

Thus the study of institutions almost always begins with or is dominated by *British Political Institutions*, central and local government, and nowadays parties and pressure groups too. We must know well the place from which we set out, and not assume we know it. This is not ethnocentrism, it is simply common sense. We have no standard of comparison otherwise. 'What do you know of England who only England know?' Point taken, but you have to know 'England', or rather the institutions and nature of the United Kingdom first. Even Karl Marx famously said, 'If you would change the world you must first understand it.'

It must be admitted that sometimes British Government is taught in a wholly descriptive and intellectually sleep-provoking manner. The teacher may not go beyond the structures to show institutions as living entities adapting, well or badly, to social change. Too few teachers in these fact-filled subjects make a serious attempt to think through what is best looked up in a reference book or textbook and what needs some explaining in class; but then, of course, the lazy student likes to have *everything* given out in lecture notes. Most teachers now, however, either attempt, on the one hand, to say something about the history of an institution and, on the other, about its likely future (i.e. to discuss reform – even if just as an intellectual hypothesis); or else they are influenced by something called 'the political culture approach', developed in the United States in the 1960s by authors like Almond, Apter, Dahl and Easton and first presented in this country by the textbooks of Richard Rose. This sought to reinterpret institutions so that they were no longer seen as legal entities (in the old days often taught by a specialist in constitutional law), but rather as a process linking policy to 'culture' – in the anthropologist's sense of the customs, beliefs and social structure of a whole society. This was often called the 'systems approach'. Society is conceived as a system of interrelating parts, of which politics is only one, which is to be shown as a dynamic model – and hypothetical models became much more common than actual accounts of the working of politics in society and society on politics. A 'contemporary history' school of politics achieves much the same intention less theoretically by showing how actual events of recent history impinge on an institution – parliament in the Suez or the Falklands crisis, or parliament and the rise of a third party, etc.

The same considerations apply to studying foreign governments. If your main interest is in British government and politics, generally look for places whose Introduction to British Government courses plainly contain a large element of politics, rather than those where British Government and British Politics are from the beginning taught separately, as chalk and cheese, and the student is left to do the integration. Institutions and processes are inseparable. They can only sensibly be separated for purposes of specialized, advanced study. The subject has long moved from the narrowly legalistic account of British Government that can still be found in a few old-fashioned school textbooks of the Harvey and Bather or the Benemy kind.

Perhaps the move from legal concepts to sociological ones (or from 'institutional' to 'process') went too far. Ironically, about the very time when textbooks were being rewritten and Constitutional Law was becoming only an optional part of a British Government course, or vanishing entirely in the new departments, the constitution suddenly became a political issue again.

The trouble in Northern Ireland after 1968 reminded authors of syllabuses and textbooks that all too often books and courses had actually been called Politics in England, or if, more accurately, The Government and Politics of the United Kingdom, they had still had precious little about the United Kingdom in them. They had little to say about the distinctive character of Welsh, Scottish and Northern Irish politics or about the major theme of modern British politics since the late seventeenth century, now so rashly taken for granted by the English that the books didn't even mention it: the political problem of holding together a multinational state.

Hardly had trouble in Ireland returned, which should have been at least intellectually stimulating in that it produced such hitherto un-British things as a constitutional convention, proportional representation and a referendum (albeit limited to Ulster), when separatist sentiment began to grow in Scotland. When the Scottish National party got nearly a third of the votes in the 1974 general election, 'devolution' was promised if 40 per cent of the electorate in a Scottish referendum so wished. That deliberately stiff hurdle was narrowly missed. But the problem remains. And there was the 1975 United Kingdom referendum on membership of the

Common Market with the famous 'agreement to differ' that had cabinet ministers arguing publicly on both sides.

Much serious opinion has come to believe that if there were a series of hung parliaments, the only way of governing the country would be through electoral reform; but it would come, like the changes in Northern Ireland, as a reaction to a problem of attempting to carry on government in an acceptable manner, not as a product of abstract reasoning and popular agitation. The possibility of a quasi-federal United Kingdom is not absurd. Many believe that a written constitution, a constitutional court and a Bill of Rights may be the only way to ensure that party majorities govern in a way that is acceptable.

Political problems have recently made the conventions of the constitution politically contentious. Some of the old lore of constitutional law, discarded in the name of what now appears as a rather academic and parochial 'realism', has had to be relearned and smuggled back into nooks and crannies of modernized syllabuses. Yet too few British Government courses really make the government and politics of the United Kingdom the centre of the picture. Not surprisingly departments like Strathclyde, Glasgow, Edinburgh, Queen's Belfast and Cardiff are among the prominent exceptions. Of course English universities always recognized that the local government and the public administration of Scotland and Northern Ireland were different, and *therefore* did not study it.

Policy studies and public administration

Public Administration is usually taught separately from British Government, as a specialized aspect of that general field. It examines the practices, methods and law relating to government administration and public boards and is thus very much a study of the working of the Civil Service – of administrators and sometimes for administrators. In some polytechnics this has become the core of a Politics course. There is naturally overlap and often some joint course with Business Studies, Management Studies and Applied Economics. In part this reflects allied academic interests, but it also indicates how the Civil Service itself has moved towards 'efficiency management' and business criteria and away from the old general administrator serving 'the public interest'.

A lot of teaching in 'Pub. Admin.' used to focus on the organization and methods of the Civil Service itself and of the local government service. It drew on Applied Economics especially in considering the problem of how to measure efficiency in the public service generally and in nationalized industries especially. Now, of course, there is the debate about privatization, its methods and effectiveness; and a continuing debate about the organization and financing of the Health Service. The Health Service has always posed an especially difficult problem for administrators and a fascinating one for students: the intrinsic difficulty of controlling expenditure when doctors and public demand the best in modern medicine at a time of rapid technological advance and an ageing population. Public Administration also involves Public Law and, specifically, Adminstrative Law – those aspects of law and the whole structure of tribunals outside the normal courts which have to deal with problems arising from the exercise of administrative discretion. The introduction of the 'Ombudsman', or Parliamentary Commissioner was a famous attempt to deal with people's grievances which arise simply from maladministration, rather than any actual breach of the law.

Sometimes 'Policy Studies' is simply a sexy name for Public Administration, an old dog bluffing through new tricks. The area of overlap is great but there is a significantly different direction of thrust and intent, if the names are used helpfully. The distinction is broadly between the *how* and the *what* of administration. Politics itself can be simply reactive and conciliatory, dealing with problems and conflicts that occur. Administration can similarly be reactive and retentive of an existing system. Good administration, as it were, need not show: a government department or a school, whatever it is, should run smoothly without disputes about how it is done. Administrators should administer. They should not, according to the traditional view, make policy, and there need not be any policy at all other than that of keeping the ship afloat, living within one's means and dealing objectively with rules relating to the allocation of resources. But 'policy' is a continued attempt to obtain some premeditated goal for the public good (or one which is believed to be so). Policy has an object beyond simply maintaining an institution.

The political theorist must help by reminding us that the very idea of 'state policy' is no older than the Renaissance. Most government was reactive, keeping the peace and defending the realm, and any innovations were thought to be a matter of royal or dynastic will, not of state policy with external, rational criteria defining a presumed public interest. Strong kings were thought of as intervening within a traditional system, not of trying to achieve something new and permanent by modifying part of that system. When policy emerges society is moving, in Weber's terms, from a world of traditional or of charismatic authority, into a 'rational legal order'.

In a 'rational legal order' bureaucrats not merely become important as instruments of policy but as contributors, at least, to its making. Loyalty to the state is not enough. Training and qualifications become important and politically contentious. Indeed loyalty to 'the state' rather than to the person of the monarch marks a stage in the development of both bureaucracy (using that term quite neutrally to mean a profession of administration) and the idea of public policy itself.

So Policy Studies covers both the formation of policy (policy-making) and the implementation of policy. Monitoring the results of legislation used to be badly done, if at all, both in Whitehall and the universities and polytechnics. For example, a new body of legislation passes through parliament to control land use, the Town and Country Planning Act 1968, say. The origins of the movement and what led to the passage of the legislation would be studied. But there would be little subsequent attempt to study whether it worked or not! To tell whether something works, it is necessary to define its objectives reasonably clearly, and then to devise tests and measures for, as we now say, monitoring performance. Only recently has this begun both in the public service and in academic research.

Monitoring performance is especially difficult in relation to particular social services, let alone to the idea of a welfare state in general. There are so many intangibles: can 'performance' and client or consumer 'satisfaction' be measured? The whole idea of monitoring performance is relatively new, and obviously it has become closely linked with ideas of public and parliamentary accountability. In France particularly, 'efficiency audits' are regularly conducted on public bodies by an independent department of state. In Britain the Comptroller and Auditor General is still mainly concerned with accounting, with whether expenditures are authorized, and only moves slowly into broader considerations of 'value for money'.

These kinds of question move a long way from traditional Public Administration. And they link this part of Politics very closely to Social Administration and Applied Economics. The questions can be great ones: the desirability and feasibility of social policies themselves (also foreign policy-making and financial and industrial policy formation). And until the *aims* of secondary education are more clear, how can the effectiveness of different structures and of individual teachers be measured? Or is there a danger to liberty itself in trying to make these things too clear and thus rigid?

Most students of Policy Studies would not think that that was their question, but the late Richard Titmus, a great reforming Professor of Social Administration, was deeply concerned with 'liberty' in relation to 'discretion' in the Supplementary Benefit Commission. Should field officers and counter-staff have discretion, so that the supplementary benefit can meet the needs of very different individual cases? If they should, what training is appropriate? And how can the effectiveness of a social worker be assessed? Titmus was also concerned by how different moral assumptions in societies affect administration. His book *The Gift Relationship* (1971) was a kind of administrative parable: the NHS greatly benefits by entirely voluntary and free donations of blood, whereas American hospital costs are inflated by the need to purchase every drop. And, of course, the exercise of discretion at the counter, as well as public policy itself, is greatly affected by common values and assumptions about 'deserving cases' or 'welfare scroungers'. Some people now try to develop the idea of 'welfare rights' as necessary to modern citizenship. Policy Studies can thus create unexpected conjuctions of Political Philosophy and Public Administration.

Three university departments view Policy Studies as the core of an undergraduate degree. Essex concentrates on trying to show what the social sciences could contribute to public policy formation over a wide range of special topics, and offers training in statistical and investigative techniques. Brunel offers similar training but puts more stress on case studies of actual processes of administration, which fits in well with the general Brunel policy of a 'sandwich' or work experience year. At Strathclyde, Policy Studies is the major postgraduate and research concentration and if, strictly speaking, the undergraduate Politics syllabus is a good main-line balance of institutions, ideas and politics, yet 'public policy formation' seems a red-thread running through most of the syllabus. Public Policy or Public Administration is much more common as a major component of a Politics degree in the polytechnics: Leicester, Manchester, Sheffield, Teesside, Trent and the Polytechnic of Wales all offer full degrees.

Parties and pressure groups

Party is the main institution in the modern world that attempts to control and conduct government. One of the most fundamental distinctions is between regimes of one-party government and multi-party government. Prejudice in this country seems still to think that two-party systems are somehow best and natural, but that is nonsense. Party systems reflect more than they shape different national histories, changing belief systems and social structures.

The distinctively modern study of Politics really began with writers in the 1920s and 1930s who accepted the centrality of party. The pioneering work was in a purely historical mode, M.A. Ostrogorski's *Democracy and the Organisation of Political Parties* (1902), an examination of the effect of the Second Reform Bill in Great Britain, which for the first time had created a mass franchise and consequently national party organization outside parliament. Robert Michels in his more sociological *Political Parties* (1915) concluded from study of the German Socialist party that there was 'an iron law of oligarchy' that gradually moved control of democratic movements from the base to the apex, or rather to a class of permanent officials. The problem of 'bureaucratization' was born.

Sometimes parties are taught as part of British Government or British Government and Politics courses, sometimes as a separate subject. The American style of studying Politics 'scientifically', using as much measurement and/or model-building (as in Economics) as possible, was especially influential in the development of the study of parties. American research furnished a lot to measure, and many models of party systems and their attributes or functions could be developed. In the 1960s this had considerable impact in Great Britain. Only two new departments ever constructed their whole syllabus on such assumptions, Essex under Jean Blondel and Strathclyde under Richard Rose (though the latter department is now more open-minded and eclectic). Most departments simply added a new believer or an American-trained adept, typically teaching the old parties course renamed as The Political Process. As in the rebirth of Public Administration as Policy Science, sometimes this meant something new and serious, sometimes it was window-dressing or old wine in new bottles.

Although the prejudices of British teachers of Politics are more inclined to historical than to behavioural or 'scientific' explanations, there has been a strange lack of major work on the history of the parties. Apart from R.T. McKenzie's once famous *British Political Parties* (1964) (now both badly dated and revealed as a much more partisan book than it seemed at the time), there is nothing on party to parallel the late John Mackintosh's *The British Cabinet* (1981). Mackintosh's book is overwhelmingly historical because he thought that the only sensible explanation of how the present-day cabinet came to be what it is. Of what has been written, much more has appeared on the origins of the Labour party than on the modern Conservative party. Most Conservative historians seem to favour biography more than thematic or institutional history.

Only Samuel H. Beer's *Modern British Politics* (1965) came near to establishing the past categories of thought that underlay the alternatives in our modern system: he identified five theories of representation and their institutional forms: the old Tory, the old Whig, Liberal and radical politics, and the two varieties of collectivism: socialism and Tory democracy. Now that the Conservative party has seemingly become 'liberal' and individualistic in Beer's terms and has broken from the collectivist consensus of the welfare state politics of the post-1945 decades, it is interesting to reflect on whether his theory needs drastic reformulation or whether we simply say that any general theory in politics is relative to particular times and circumstances.

Pressure groups are usually studied together with parties and there is a rather inconclusive debate about their relative importance, or simply about how one best conceptualizes their relationship. Beyond that, pressure groups need to be studied case by case. Many good case studies of pressure groups have been made, as well as various attempts to categorize them according to their purpose or method of working. There is a general belief that pressure groups have recently grown *relatively* more important than parties in policy formulation in Britain. But studies of the great Victorian railway lobby by political scientists make this, indeed, a very qualified and relative conclusion. The situation is very different in the United States. Some conceptual frameworks, developed in American conditions where the articulation of parties is weak and of pressure groups is strong, were transplanted to British conditions too uncritically. S.E. Finer's *Anonymous Empire: a study of the lobby in Britain* (1966), though now badly dated in content, is still the best attempt to provide an intellectual framework for studying pressure groups of a British kind in British conditions.

Much good work on pressure groups occurs in Sociology and in Modern History, and is often taught as Political Sociology or, depending on the subject matter, as part of Comparative Politics. The objects of pressure groups and lobbies are easier to define precisely than the vastly more comprehensive objectives of political parties. Therefore it is more easy to compare like with like across cultural boundaries. Most comparisons of political parties between nations, however, are either very abstract and specious or else end up admitting that party in one culture can mean something very different in another. This has become true even for the one case where there was an international and a highly centralized political party, the Communist party.

The study of elections and public opinion is sometimes part of Parties and Pressure Groups, but is sometimes singled out. There can be separate courses in Survey Methods or in Methodology of Political Science, which can have a somewhat similar practical side. Two departments have great fame in this, again Essex and Strathclyde. The Nuffield Election Studies series came out of Nuffield College, Oxford, but had little influence on the BA degree syllabus. For a time at Essex and Strathclyde there seemed a deliberate intent to train all students in such statistical techniques of investigation. The concentration is still heavy and still available, but somehow the importance of it all now seems less than was once thought, or perhaps its intellectual respectability is now so well-established as part of the study that its innovations and new ideas are now relatively small and technical. The political debate is now more about the use and abuse of opinion polls rather than about their accuracy.

Concentration among the 'dogmatic empiricists' (I mean people who are determined to study problems because of their measurability rather than their importance) has noticeably moved from Electoral Studies to Policy Studies. Sheer cost has precluded 'longitudinal' or generational studies of what is ambitiously called 'political attitude formation', which could have given new life to a well-worked subject. Certainly there is a link between Policy Studies and public response and acceptability which is as yet little explored, and has little to do with voting behaviour as such.

It is fair to say that the best training in research on social and political attitudes and on survey methodology is often to be found in Sociology departments. Every student of Politics needs to know more than most about public opinion as it has been measured, and to have a critical awareness of sources and methods; but relatively few will need to learn the techniques of investigation – except in so far as a general knowledge of the techniques available helps weigh the worth of published or on-line data-bank evidence.

'Cross-polity surveys' were developed, famously, in Almond and Verba's *The Civic Culture* (1963). These are interesting both to the political theorist and the political sociologist, but the comparability of some of the samples remains very dubious – not merely do key words in questions have different connotations in different cultures but also acceptance of and resistance to polling itself varies greatly.

Comparative government and politics

Every department has it but no subsection of the subject can vary more widely in its content. In some it would simply be better called Some Modern Foreign Governments. Invariably courses on the USA are offered, often on the USSR, usually some attempt is made to teach not the politics of the European Economic Community and its member states (a very tall order indeed) but the main structure of the common institutions – the commission, the parliament and the court etc. In other departments institutions and functions of government are studied across a potentially wide range of countries. 'Party' can be looked at comparatively, and so can organizational concepts like 'communication', 'participation' and, of course, 'democracy' itself, 'representative institutions' and 'nationalism'. So Comparative Government and Politics can look very much like Political Theory (as generalization and explanation) in the way that I tried to distinguish it from Political Philosophy as conceptual analysis or justification. Or it may study some particular movement or sect and examine variations in different cultural settings, in a manner hard or impossible to distinguish from what is often taught as Political Sociology. Hardly surprisingly there is a growing literature on terrorism, just as in the post-war generation there was on Nazism.

Some teaching on Comparative Government is obsessed with problems of classification. Some extraordinary scientific-sounding nomenclatures have been produced in an attempt to escape from the 'political' overtones of terms like 'democracy', 'autocracy' and 'totalitarian'. But all classifications, if they are to put like together with like and separate out unlike from unlike, must make assumptions or be explicit theories: they are not just coat hooks, they work like a sorting machine. The problem of 'names' is a classic dilemma in the social sciences: to use common names is, in some ways, to risk misunderstanding (as in the way I distinguish 'theory' and 'doctrine'), but to invent *allegedly* value-free names (i.e. neologisms like 'polyarchy' and 'consociationalism' – which is how multicultural, bi-national Belgium is governed) is to invite incomprehension, and simply trap the student in a web of definitions rather than of empirical generalizations.

There is something to be said for the Some Foreign Governments Approach, so long as they are not too many. To know another country's politics almost as well as one's own (though the difficulties are formidable, for it involves another history, culture and usually *should* involve another language) is not merely an enriching experience compared to skimming over the tops of a score of peaks, but is probably a transferable skill. If I really steeped myself in French or German politics, and I then got a job in Italy, the new learning experience would probably be easier than if I had known just a little about Italy in advance and thought I knew more. Diplomats can move from post to post; they know how to learn by analogy; and this is likely to be a better system than that of trying to gain a general training in Comparative Government under Professor X at the University of Y. This set of considerations makes Area Studies programmes very attractive to some, or to others simply points to a joint degree in Politics and a modern language.

However, some movements – like Communism – are or were genuinely international, and some problems are almost universal and can benefit by comparison. And governments (and peoples?) can feel affinities towards each other as well as mutual interest if they feel that they have 'institutions and values in common'. This cliché does have meaning. Up to a point there are institutions and values in common between countries, but there are never identical twins. A widely read book, Professor S.E. Finer's *Comparative Government* (1974) identified three main forms of modern government, 'Liberal–Democracy', 'Totalitarianism' and 'Autocracy and Oligarchy', but gave concrete examples of particular governments. This was an interesting pedagogic compromise between the general (but often too abstract) and the specific (from which no generalizations can be made).

Some syllabuses deal with regional groupings. Teaching of Third World Politics is still very popular despite the fact that often 'Third World' countries have very little in common, and the whole concept of 'underdevelopment' is intellectually very dubious. It assumes a common pattern of necessary development towards something like Western industrial society. This can be challenged on moral and political grounds quite as much as historical ones. Theory is piled upon theory when one seeks to explain why The Politics of Developing Nations should attribute the same form of development to each nation, or if not, what the different countries in such a course have in common except a Western perception of their poverty or of our guilt. People teaching the course attest that they are not 'ethnocentric', not imposing our Western values on 'Third World' cultures, but then too often go on to impose Western economic history. (This is what philosophers call the fallacy of teleology, the belief that everything has an inherent purpose and goal.)

A substantial element of common culture can justify The Politics of Sub-Saharan Africa or of South-East Asia; but 'Third World', 'development' and 'underdevelopment' are concepts one must approach carefully with some of the scepticism as well as the evaluative intent of political philosophy. That we rightly think that poverty and a history of oppression create some similar political responses, some common needs and that the richer nations *should* be doing more about it, does not imply any common culture or political system.

The 'communications age' has spawned the concept of the 'global village'; yet this at best assumes, and at worst imposes, a false community of values. It is better to be honestly evaluative than to smuggle in undiscussed values while we pretend to be objective and invent, as a mental construct, common cultures so that we can be objective and scientific about them. At this point the circle turns either to link Comparative Politics with Political Theory and Philosophy, or to admit that it is International Relations that really concerns one.

International relations

International Relations is sometimes a separate subject or sometimes an option or group of options within a Politics degree. In some ways it would seem extraordinary that the two can even exist apart. Foreign policy and domestic policy are obviously closely related, and it is hardly possible to understand British politics without understanding the commitments of Britain in the outside world and also the restraints that come from the outside world – economic, military and political. None the less there is a vital theoretical difference between politics *within* a state and politics *between* states. Within a state, if at the end of the day a political compromise cannot be found, a decision can be enforced – by the state itself. Politics is conducted in that knowledge. In the international relations of states there is no sovereign body. That is the main problem. As Hobbes said, states stand 'like armed gladiators' against each other. In domestic politics the state normally has a monopoly of politically effective arms – otherwise it is civil war.

The study has three components: relations between states; the character of international institutions; and theories or models which seek to link the first two components. The balance can be struck very differently in different departments. Some are virtually International History, with a great deal not merely about diplomacy but also about the actual course of the diplomatic relations of the Great Powers. But others are mainly theoretical, almost a branch of Political Theory and Political Philosophy: the nature of international order, the senses in which there is international law or not, and models of structures or processes.

Those places which offer virtually a whole degree in International Relations obviously allow for great choice and specialization, mainly geographical. Probably the smaller the course or number of papers, the more it will focus on the United Nations Organization – not perhaps because of its power and importance but simply as a pedagogically convenient focus for the study. Sometimes Strategic Studies or Defence Studies are offered as courses (though such considerations tend to run through everything else) and sometimes Peace Studies or Conflict Resolution.

Four big problems tend to dominate the syllabus, each of which can affect domestic or national politics but cannot possibly be contained or resolved except by international co-operation: (i) arms control; (ii) the dislocation and uncertainty of the present world economic system; (iii) the North–South divide, both in terms of wealth, poverty, population and military muscle; and (iv) global ecological and environmental problems. And, of course, we now have the power, as the unintended consequences of both economic and military actions, to destroy the habitable environment.

There is a lot to be said for a joint honours degree in Politics and International Relations, as several places offer. Indeed, as I've said, however important and interesting the subject of Politics itself, any student should consider seriously both the possible intellectual and occupational advantage of pursuing two subjects rather than one, even if they are not integrated.

7

Nice combinations

More people take *History and Politics* than any other degree combination. 'History without Politics has no fruit, Politics without History has no root', the old tag has it. The American style of statistical studies and model-building fits in badly with History in a curriculum; but the British style of balance between 'institutions and ideas' (with just a few gestures at bridging them) is closer to History. Even within the Labour movement more can be explained by invoking tradition than by objective measures of income and social class etc. It depends, of course, more than a little on what is on offer in a particular History department. Some modern History courses or topics will be very close to central preoccupations of Politics – something like The Age of Revolutions obviously, or more specialist studies of the American, French or Russian Revolutions, the Nazi period, the causes of the two World Wars etc. Remember that many or most dual degrees are not integrated, they are half of each. Sussex, notably, and many of the new institutions try to present integrated courses; but the resulting demand on staff time limits the number of combinations any department can offer. Personally, I think there is a lot to be said for having two strings to one's bow. But look for History departments that show some sign of thought, that are not just a string of 'special periods' one after the other but also have thematic and comparative courses.

Economics is the next most popular combination with Politics. The intellectual justification for the combination is formidable. Several of the older chairs in Economics are called Political Economy, a reminder of the eighteenth and early nineteenth centuries when no one imagined that the two sets of considerations could ever be studied apart. The view that

Politics is meaningless without Economics is held at opposite points of the political spectrum: both Marxists and liberals of *laissez-faire* persuasion speak of Political Economy, though they reach different practical considerations. Most of us believe that Politics can sensibly be studied on its own, and that political factors should be some limit on the market. But equally political policies need to be economically realistic, and it is hard to see how studies of policy formation can be pursued meaningfully without some knowledge of Economics. Be sure that you are numerate enough however to cope with a particular Economics course.

Sociology is also a fairly popular option. Some people are eager to see the whole of Politics as a relationship between different social factors. Sociology departments vary in content and outlook even more than Politics departments. So if you hunt for a dual degree, look as carefully at the Sociology side of the line as you should at the Politics. Some are very theoretical – all Marx, Durkheim, and Weber, which can go well with Political Theory. Others are very empirical and are all about contemporary social structure, measures of class, mobility and population, which can go well with British Government or Policy Studies. Women's Studies are often part of such a combination, but no dual degree in Women's Studies and Politics is yet available. Political Sociology can be taught and is taught in either department. Strictly speaking the Sociology of Politics and Political Sociology should at least be different emphases; but the terms are used by most people as if they were identical.

Philosophy can only be and should be the combination for those who think of themselves as political philosophers. Within even the most philosophical of Politics degrees, as can be the case still at Oxford and LSE above most others (certainly in numbers of teachers and courses), there is little time or space for Philosophy of Knowledge, Mind, Logic or Ethics. The good political philosopher needs something of this. To have read Aristotle's *Politics* but not the *Ethics* is, alas, to know only half the story. Even the best History of Political Thought courses commonly have to ignore Kant and Hume and deal briefly if at all with Hegel, three of the most important philosophers of our tradition. And you may never learn what Wittgenstein was on about, a figure as important in shaping our modern consciousness as Marx and Freud. But beware that most philosophers are very dedicated and demanding, you require a very sharp, quick and analytical mind – you don't actually need to play chess but it helps.

There are many other combinations available, some of the most interesting of which, both intellectually and vocationally, can be found among 'Politics with a foreign language'. Language students have, in the last 20 years, waged a steady and fairly successful campaign to get their teachers to include some social studies as well as literature and language in their courses. But languages are usually taken as a follow-on from studying the language at school. Some places allow you to start a language from scratch (especially Spanish – which opens up the whole of Latin American politics), but then it could be a struggle all the way and you'd usually be at a disadvantage. You could, however, do something real heavy where everyone is in the same boat, Soviet Studies, for instance, or Japanese and Politics. And some places allow a combination of Politics and English. That can be very pleasant and vocationally sensible for those who look towards a career in the media or in publishing of any form. It is the one I often wish I could have done. But then, never forget, a good subject should make you want to radiate out in your reading – if not in the next three or four years, then later. Intellectual life does go on after graduation, if ever it begins; and all subject divisions are pretty arbitrary both to the thinking mind and in their application in the outside world.

Appendices

These Appendices are designed to be of help to you in seeing what types of course are on offer, and in deciding which institution best suits your personal requirements. The information contained is necessarily limited and we would strongly recommend that once a range of possible places has been decided, that you send away for individual departmental prospectuses (or sometimes you'll get one for a whole faculty or the combined degree programmes). These will give you the fine print and detail, and you'll thereby discover what it is exactly you are letting yourself in for!

Appendix A: General advice on applications

The UCCA scores of successful candidates tell the usual story of the attraction of geography mixed with the sometimes rather garbled reputations for being good at the subject.

The Times Higher Educational Supplement, 5 Feb. 1983

Now that you have made the decision to study in the area of Politics and International Relations, the hardest choice is yet to be made. At which noble seat of learning should I further my education and for which particular course should I apply?

Often this decision is taken in an uninformed and haphazard manner. Friends, relations or teachers are often ready with free advice drawn from their own experience, yet the danger is that this advice may be out of date. The eager young lecturers they studied under are now at least a lot older and often elsewhere. Things do change. Vague notions of a particular place's general reputation or environmental splendour, or otherwise, often outweigh questions of individual department excellence or the precise nature of the course to be studied. For several reasons, this is not necessarily such a bad thing, nevertheless it is our contention that while many personal, non-academic factors may hold considerable sway in finally opting for a particular university, polytechnic or college, yet it is important to be well acquainted with the particular departmental course details.

When one arrives one does not want to find oneself in the position of studying in a completely unexpected and unsuitable manner. Besides, a bit of prior preparation takes the pressure off marvellously when you do arrive and makes life far less hectic.

Academic considerations The study of Politics can be approached in many different ways and covers a wide range of topics. Under its broad title various orientations of study can lie. From political philosophy to strategic studies or to the contemporary policy-making process, the range of departmental specialisms is wide. Whilst it is true that the great majority of medium- or large-sized departments are able to offer options from the whole spectrum, it may prove useful to have some knowledge of where particular course strengths and weaknesses lie. For example, whereas departments at Essex, Strathclyde, Leeds and the London School of Economics are all able to offer a wide range of courses, the first two are noted for their psephology (statistical analysis of voting behaviour) and empirical attitude research, whereas LSE specializes in political philosophy. Indeed, if it is political philosophy you are after, don't go to Essex or Strathclyde, or if it is voting and attitude research, LSE would not be the most obvious choice. We mention Leeds as just typical of a middle-sized department with no great international reputation and few famous 'specialities of the house' but with good solid teaching strength and scholarship all through: one could just as well have mentioned Bristol, Edinburgh, Exeter, Glasgow, Hull, Kent, Lancaster, Liverpool, Queen's Belfast, Sheffield, Southampton, Swansea, Warwick and York; or Birmingham, Bradford, Central London, City of London, Kingston and Thames among the polys.

Thus you must initially ask yourself what your purpose or interest is in studying Politics and what particular area of strength, if any, you might prefer. If you decide that your reason for studying Politics is to pursue, for example, a career in local government administration, then you should look seriously at some of the more vocationally orientated polytechnic courses, rather than just using them as a fall-back. If your interests are less vocational and are concentrated on global security, then a course leaning towards international relations, peace studies or strategic studies could be for you. However, if your purpose is less certain, and you are perhaps only looking for a pleasant place to take a good general degree, then more wide-ranging considerations such as the overall quality of a department, the range of courses available and non-academic factors will be more important.

One factor of some concern to new students may be the department's assessment technique. It is as well to understand in advance how you are to be examined in order to avoid the frustration of feeling that you are being 'unfairly' assessed. The majority of departments now offer, in very varying proportions to the whole, some form of continuous assessment – sometimes optional, sometimes compulsory and always, of course, for essays, projects or course work, never for performance in class or in oral examination. The percentage of the final degree that is, or can be, derived from continuous assessment varies widely. A few places still offer the traditional three-hour written examinations taken all together at the end, or sometimes with a few in the second year. But the trend is towards some combination of the two methods and a spread between second and third year.

In the 1970s there was strong and effective student pressure in most places against the then all but universal system of three-hour papers and 'all your eggs in one basket'. But not all students agreed then, or now. Some see continuous assessment as continual surveillance and prefer an undisturbed second year to read and think widely without the nagging worries and the often narrowing effects of known exams. So always check to find what the system is before you commit yourself and try to think out which is likely to suit you best. Also remember, just a tip, that performance in class can be very important for that final form of 'assessment' that is rarely if ever discussed, but which can do a lot to make up for a disappointing degree result or to make sure that a good one is noticed: the tutor's reference. When you apply for jobs this can carry a lot of weight, do a lot to make up for a disappointing result or to make sure that a good one sits up and is noticed.

Many courses now offer as an option, and some require, a dissertation or extended essay. These can vary in length from 8,000 to 15,000 words (there are about 300 words on an average double-spaced typed page, look at it that way; or this whole book is about 30,000 words). They can be a source of great pain or great satisfaction (sometimes a mixture of both). If this prospect is terrifying, avoid places where the prospectus shows they are compulsory.

A point often stressed in department prospectuses is size. A typical self-promotional line might read: 'With X teaching staff and Y students, you will find your department large enough to offer a wide range of courses and variety, yet small enough to be friendly and accessible.' Again, this is a question of taste and temperament. But as a personal opinion I would not place too much significance on department size. Provided that the courses on offer are what you want, departments generally are what you make of them. As a generalization, the larger the department may be, the more impersonal it feels, whilst the smaller ones can perhaps be claustrophobic. Staff–student relations depend as much on the students as on the staff, and as a rule you will find that if you are prepared to 'bother' people you will nearly always find them amenable whatever the size of the department (within the constraints of their own personalities, of course – most departments seem to have at least one ancient member who has grown to hate the place and everyone connected with it, and another who tries to stay young for ever by doing nothing but drink beer with the students).

Another serious consideration is the possibility of interdisciplinary study in the first year. Most places now offer a first year in which Politics can be combined with one or two other subjects, normally drawn from either the social science or the arts faculties. As well as being useful in broadening your horizons and keeping your options open, such courses are advisable in as much as they can provide a useful escape route if you find that Politics disagrees with you and you would like to move sideways into another discipline. (Politics usually gains more than it loses in these transactions; it speaks well for the subject that it can grow on people.) Departments do not always candidly advertise the possibilities for such transfers in their brochures, yet with a mixed first year this is usually possible if you are firm; and the fine print of university or faculty regulations may be more supportive than the bold promotional print of department brochures – often with a pretty picture of someone climbing in the Pennines or bathing in the Channel. Some universities and all polytechnics simply assume that what you do at school cannot possibly be a clear enough guide to what you would be letting yourself in for in honours work, and therefore the whole first year is structured less as a stumbling block, less even as sequential instruction, and more as a shop window for several social sciences to help you make the big choice that matters at the end of year one. After all some schools hardly teach social sciences at all, and few if any teach Anthropology, Psychology and Law.

Another possibility is that of taking a joint or dual honours degree, or a multi-disciplinary combined degree as is the norm in almost all polytechnics. Note that the Scottish universities all have four-year courses for honours, and have a very wide spread of subjects in the first year (they are, of course, open to applicants from anywhere else in the United Kingdom). The mixed-disciplinary nature of Politics lends itself particularly well to combinations with other subjects. History, Economics, Sociology and Philosophy being the most common companions, with many other weird and wonderful combinations being available. Politics and English, for example, is possible at a few places, which can make a lot of sense if you were aiming at career in journalism, broadcasting or publishing.

Check the UCCA and the PCAS handbooks for what combinations are available. While such dual courses are often accused of generating excessive work loads, there is no reason why joint studies should not prove to be more interesting to some than single honours. The examination arrangements in joint schools are usually very carefully watched by faculties to avoid overload (that is, expecting the students of joint honours to know as much as those doing single); and sometimes (we suspect) joint honours degrees are subject to 'disinformation campaigns' by members of staff who may want the better students wholly in their most precious subject. Careerwise a dual honours programme can make good sense, such as combinations with a modern language. Some mean by Politics and Economics, for instance, an attempt to integrate the two subjects, or to study just the points where they touch; but most combinations are, in fact, 'chalk and cheese', and possibly the better for it, unless the staff themselves are genuinely interdisciplinary. With chalk and cheese at least you know the real nature of two different disciplines.

As we have stressed, at the risk of repetition, it is extremely important to have a good knowledge of the details of the courses you might like to follow. Three years can be wasted, or could have been better spent, if the initial decision is not taken carefully. If you can take a year out between school and further study (which we think is a *very* good idea) use part of it to familiarize yourself with the options, both of where to go and what to do when there. Do a lot of writing around, however wise and knowledgable your careers teacher or parent might seem. And, of course, the success of your study is not wholly dependent on the academic merits of your department. There are, indeed, non-academic factors that need to be taken into consideration.

Non-academic considerations As someone nearly said somewhere, three years is a long time in Politics. Even with the highest motivation and the most interesting course, taught by teachers as if it is all fresh, urgent and exciting, environmental considerations can still spoil your stay. It is extremely important to make sure that the place you finally decide upon is pleasant enough to live in. After all, it is harder to work in disagreeable surroundings. The figures show (or, as they say in the jargon you'll learn, 'empirical evidence suggests') that most students elect to study in a town between 100 and 200 miles from their home-base. This isn't so much a reflection on our island's geography, as a sign that most people like to get away from home, but not too far. (Newcastle, for instance, has more than the odd Scot.) It is hard to decide which towns are more pleasant to live in, especially after only a brief glance on a rainy day (but that's better than nothing). It is not my place to make value judgements that would get us sued by town clerks as well as vice-chancellors and directors. However, to visit the towns is highly to be recommended. Even a quick look at a place can tell you more about its atmosphere and real location than can the glossy promotion photographs.

   Institutions that are integrated into the town rather than way out of the town (even if carrying the famous name of the town) tend to be more popular, but again it is a matter of taste. When the new universities were new they were very popular, though nearly all in parkland sites outside the city, some remarkably far outside. Inner city renewal has clawed back a lot of once lost 'well-qualified' candidates to the old civic universities. Don't be inhibited by regional preconceptions. Some northern towns whose very names sound grim to southern ears turn out to have restored and lively inner cities and beautiful hinterlands (so much more interesting than home in London when 'London' usually means the suburbs). The best departments are by no means always found in the traditionally favoured gracious university towns. We said we wouldn't make endorsements, but *if* we were talking about History, then one of the greatest History schools for many years has been Manchester. That is a name that does not 'warm the blood like wine', but the town has a range of cultural facilities and a civic pride in them – theatre, music, art galleries and libraries, as well as the modern scene – that can only be matched outside London by Edinburgh, Glasgow and possibly Bristol.

   If you have a particular interest you wish to pursue on the side, be it korfball, origami, climbing or drama, it is well worth consulting the Student Unions' handbooks to see what societies and facilities exist. Some Student Unions also publish some form of 'Alternative Prospectus', a guide book written for students by students which can also give useful information on such matters, and sometimes a less formal, student's-eye view of academic matters. Don't attach too much weight to these, as they are only personal viewpoints, but they can provide useful indicators. We don't list any because they are so spasmodic. Even places that try to update them regularly don't always get their act together in time. But it is worth asking if there is one as you begin to narrow the field.

   So choosing one's place is, or should be, quite a complex process. Notions of academic quality and course content are important, but so are questions of environment. If a friend or relative went to a particular place, enjoyed it and has stayed in touch, this might well be as good a reason as any for deciding to go there (we could have put that on a postcard and not written a book); always provided that you have acquainted yourself with the kind of course you will be doing and the town you will be living in for three or (in Scotland) four years. Take the decision seriously, and you are unlikely to be disappointed.

   So far I have been talking slightly glibly as if the world is everyone's oyster. Sadly this is not so, and your applications are necessarily limited by your probable or actual examination results. It is possible, more or less, to discover what grades different places and departments demand; so you will have some idea of where it is feasible to apply.

The general rule is to put the most prestigious place on your list first, even if it is not your actual top preference (which you might rank second or third). Some snobby places only look at the top of the list, they have so many applications.* Remember you have five choices, so use them all wisely. Don't lose interest in the brochures and visiting (if at all possible) when you get to your fourth and fifth bids.

A common mistake made by those applying through UCCA who have spread their five bids through the middle and lower ranges of requirements, is to fail to look at what is on offer at the polys. Do not be caught by this status trap. Polytechnics do not merely provide a fall-back if university entrance is unsuccessful. In many cases the standards of teaching are equally good, and often better organized, than at the universities. In some universities the syllabus falls together largely by historical accident, and who wants to teach what and how in a very independent-minded staff. But every polytechnic course has had to stand up and be justified according to standards of competence, content, scope, method and objectives defined by central committees of the Council for National Academic Awards (composed of both university and polytechnic teachers of great experience), and visiting parties who regularly inspect, supervise changes and consult with students as well as staff and directors.

Most university teachers scoff at this as bureaucratic and interventionist. But it makes the average standard of teaching high and leads to rationally constructed curricula. As a general rule, students in polytechnics are taught more often and more systematically. Perhaps it leaves them with less time for reading on their own, but many students welcome the more structured learning environment and can feel a bit lost in university with the abrupt change between the fully timetabled existence of the sixth form (perhaps five free periods a week – big deal!) and a typical university timetable of perhaps only five, six or seven hours a week in lecture or class rooms (based on the odd assumption that students should know how to study on their own and use a major library sensibly). As a general rule the staff in polytechnics have to teach many more hours than in university and have far less opportunity for original research. This makes them poor and unlikely places for postgraduate studies but sometimes better for the middle range of undergraduates. The CNAA also tries to ensure by external examiners that the standards of the degrees are the same as those in universities. This seems to work.

The information that follows is designed to be of some help in determining which courses are offered at what places, with some

*UCCA have announced an end to this preferential listing from 1989: candidates will be asked to list institutions alphabetically.

indicators as to how to distinguish and decide between them. Once more, don't take our word for it or anyone else's, write away for prospectuses and try to see for yourself.

Appendix B: Table of courses on offer

The official list of university courses available appears annually in the UCCA handbook and for polytechnics and other degree-awarding colleges in the PCAS handbook (see Appendix E).

The table below lists courses available at the time of going to print with their titles, length if other than three years, and degree if other than a BA or a B.Sc.; the number of full-time teaching staff (though in the polytechnics where interdisciplinary teaching is usual these figures often include many full-time staff from other areas who teach only a small part of a Politics degree); and the number of students graduating last year (when known or given) *whether single or dual honours*; and lastly the method of assessment. We think the number graduating gives you a better measure of the size of a department than the staff–student ratio used in university planning, for that figure is weighted by postgraduates, by students in other departments taught in the first year and by subsidiary courses. We are well aware that the bases of the figures that have been given to us are not always fully comparable.

First we list places and courses which offer a predominantly Politics degree. Then we list places *only* offering combined degrees. But many, perhaps most, of those in the first list also allow combinations with other honours degrees. You *must* use the UCCA handbook to establish this. (A large number of students in our table in proportion to staff is a sign of combined degrees.) The CRAC (Careers Research and Advisory Centre – a private body) *Degree Course Guide, Politics* (1985) gives some indication of the content of combined degrees (the Politics components of which can be very small), but you *must* get the syllabuses from the places when you've narrowed your list; it would be very difficult and often misleading to summarize some combined degrees – we don't try. The methods of assessment are expressed thus:

A = Written examinations only.
B = Written examinations with some continuous assessment.
C = Written examinations with substantial continuous assessment.
a = An optional dissertation that can be substituted for one or more written papers.
b = A compulsory dissertation replacing one or more written papers.

Single Politics Degrees

Univ./Poly	Course Title	Exam Mode	Staff	Nos. Graduating
Aberdeen (4 MA)	Political Studies	Aa	14	40
Aberystwyth	International Politics	Aa	10	31
	Int. Pol. & Int. History	Aa	—	—
	Int. Pol. & Strategic Studies	Aa	—	—
	Int. Pol. & Political Science	Aa	—	—
	Modern Social & Pol. Thought	Aa	—	—
	Politics	Ca	8	35
Belfast (3 or 4)	Politics	Bb	12	60
Birmingham	Political Science	C	12	60
	Public Policy & Administration	C	—	—
Birmingham Poly	Government	Ba	9	43
Bristol	Politics	Ab	10	60
Bristol Poly	Social Science (Politics)	Ca	9	44
Brunel (3 or 4)	Govt. Pol. & Modern Hist.	Ab	11	25
	Policy Studies	—	—	—
Cardiff	Politics	Ba	6	24
City of London Poly	Politics	Cb	22	70
Dundee (4 MA)	Political Science	Ca	6	32
Durham	Politics	Cb	10	57
East Anglia	Development Studies	Bb	5	45
Edinburgh (4 MA)	Politics	Ba	12	54
Essex	Government	Cb	20	88
Exeter	Politics	Aa	21	61
Glasgow (4 MA)	Politics	Ba	14	39
Hull	Politics	Cb	14	61
Keele	Politics	Aa	6	33
	International Relations	—	—	—
Kent	Politics & Government	Ba	16	48
	Politics & Int. Relations	—	—	—
Lancaster	Politics	Ba	22	66
	Politics & Int. Relations	—	—	—
Leeds	Political Studies	Ba	14	53
Leeds (4)	Pol. & Parliamentary Studies	Ba	6	15
Leicester	Politics	Ba	13	58
Leicester Poly	Public Administration	Bb	25	42
Liverpool	Pol. Theory & Institutions	Ba	13	45
Liverpool Poly	Social Studies (Politics)	Ba	9	21
London, LSE	Government	Aa	26	37
	International Relations	Aa	17	39
London, Queen Mary College (QMC)	Politics	Bb	10	35
	Politics (jointly with School of African & Oriental Studies [SOAS])	—	—	—
Manchester	Government & Political Theory	Ba	29	145
Manchester Poly	Social Sciences (Politics)	Ba	14	90
	Public Administration	Ba	12	20
Newcastle	Politics	Aa	13	70
Newcastle Poly	Govt & Public Policy	Bb	17	—
N. Staffs. Poly	Int. Relations & Pol.	C	17	92
	International Studies	C	—	—
Nottingham	Politics	Ba	7	35
Oxford	PPE (Pol., Phil. & Econ.)	Aa	48	230

Single Politics Degrees

Univ./Poly	Course Title	Exam Mode	Staff	Nos. Graduating
Poly of Wales	Public Administration	Bb	11	35
Portsmouth Poly	Politics	Ca	9	38
Reading	Politics	Ba	16	62
	Pol. & Int. Relations	—	—	—
Sheffield	Pol. Theory & Institutions	Bc	9	49
Sheffield Poly	Public Administration	Ab	22	28
Southampton	Politics	Bb	12	72
	Pol. & International Studies	—	—	—
	Comparative & Int. Studies	—	—	—
	Public & Social Admin.	—	—	—
St Andrews (4 MA)	International Relations (dual)	Bb	3	30
Stirling (4 MA)	Political Studies	Cb	7	18
Strathclyde (4 MA)	Politics	Bb	8	18
Sussex	Politics [see Combined Degrees table below]			
Swansea	Politics	Ac	14	59
Teeside Poly	Public Administration	Cb	25	30
Thames Poly	Humanities (Politics)	Ca	6	30
Trent Poly	Public Administration	Ba	24	64
Warwick	Politics	Ba	20	82
	Pol. & International Studies	Ba	—	—
York	Politics	Ba	15	52

Combined Degrees

Univ./Poly	Course Title	Exam Mode	Staff	Nos. Graduating
Aston	Society & Government	Bc	—	—
Bath	Economics & Politics	Cb	14	16
Bradford	Social Sciences (Politics)	Bb	8	28
Bradford (4)	European Studies	Bb	9	25
Cambridge	Social & Political Sciences	A	10	72
Coventry Poly	Modern Studies (Pol. & Int. Rel.)	Ba	15	42
	Modular Degree (Econ. Geog. & Pol.)	—	—	—
Ealing College of Higher Ed.	Modern European Studies	Bb	4	36
East Anglia	Economic & Social Studies	Ba	5	50
Glasgow College of Tech. (4)	Social Sciences (Politics)	Bb	27	85
Huddersfield Poly	Humanities (Politics)	C	4	48
Keele (4)	Politics, Philosophy & Econ.	Aa	6	33
Kingston Poly	Econ. Pol. & a language	Bb	6	36
Lancashire Poly	Combined Studies	Bb	9	52
London, QMC	Politics & another subject	Ab	5	24
London, Royal Holloway & Bedford	Econ. & Public Administration	Ab	7	21
	Mod. Hist., Econ. Hist. & Pol.	—	—	—
London, SOAS	Politics & another subject	B	—	—
Loughborough	Politics & another subject	Ca	7	13
Manchester Poly	Humanities/Social Studies	Ba	13	45

Combined Degrees

Univ./Poly	Course Title	Exam Mode	Staff	Nos. Graduating
Oxford Poly	Modular Degree	Bb	8	39
Plymouth Poly	Combined Studies	Bb	6	40
Poly of Central London	Modern Studies (Politics)	Ba	7	50
Poly of N. London	Modern Studies	Cb	3	38
	Contemporary European Studies	Cb	4	18
Poly of S. Bank (4)	A modern language & Int. Studies	Cb	—	27
Salford	Social Science (Pol. & Mod. Hist.)	Bb	9	24
Sunderland Poly	Combined Studies	Bb	—	—
	Social Science	Bb	—	—
Surrey (4)	Linguistics & Int. Studies	Ba	—	—
Sussex	International Relations (can be taken with African & Asian Studies English & Africa Studies European Studies Social Sciences)	Cb	6	31
	Politics (can be taken with each of the above)	Cb	10	30
Teesside Poly	Humanities	Bb	6	19
	International Relations	—	—	—
Trent Poly	Humanities (Politics)	Bb	5	15
	Modern European Studies	Bb	—	—
Ulster	Humanities (Politics)	Cb	7	43
Wolverhampton Poly	European Studies	Bb	16	21
	Humanities/Social Science	Bb	—	—

Appendix C: Notes on evaluations of departments

Any attempt to rank departments in terms of merit would be a very ticklish business. It is not merely a question of walking through a minefield of sensitivities. The real problem would lie in deciding by what criteria one is to judge the merits or demerits of a department, and then how to obtain (by reasonably fair means) reliable evidence to match these criteria. Should an institution be judged on the volume of its research output (though then what of its quality?), the quality of its staff, its teaching *reputation* (though even in secondary schools no reliable methods have been found of assessing teacher effectiveness, or agreement reached about what that might be), the amount of external research funding that it attracts, its popularity with applicants, or its contribution to the local community and the region? And who is to decide? Colleagues in other departments, the University Grants Committee (UGC) or the Department of Education and Science?

Whatever method anyone devised would have flaws in it. The UGC two years ago (as part of a cost-cutting exercise to try to make universities concentrate on their best subjects and cease to be department stores) made subject assessments by creating its own 'subject panels' who, to avoid controversy, did not announce the methods they used to reach their decisions from the paper mountain of departmental returns. One suspects a lot of conventional 'good judgement' was used. The retiring vice-chancellor of the Queen's University, Belfast, said in a speech: 'I would like to stress we are being judged on our research quality, not our record of teaching, nor on our staff–student relationship, nor on our contribution to the community.' And the research quality of some of his departments did seem to have been most unfairly judged. Also, it emerged that the rankings for Politics owed something to a piece of bibliographic research on departmental publication rates whose data-base was heavily biased towards empirical political science and under-represented political philosophy and area studies (excluding, for instance, all journals published in Ireland).

We are not ourselves, then, in the business of making such assessments and nor have any studies been made which command automatic respect. But since they were published, we relate without further comment the UGC's 'average and above' ratings for Politics from their above-mentioned 1986 assessment of all subjects. But we cannot stress too strongly that these relate only to research.

UGC ratings for research in politics departments 1986
Outstanding
 Oxford

Above Average
 Aberystwyth (Int. Pol.), Bristol, Essex, Hull, LSE, Strathclyde, Warwick

Average
 Aberdeen, Cardiff, Durham, Exeter, Glasgow, Keele, Lancaster, Liverpool, Manchester, Nottingham, Southampton, Sussex, York.

However, one solution to the hidden subjectivity of all such attempts at evaluation is to be openly subjective: to take the opinions of the largest possible number of (self-interested) experts. *The Times Higher Educational Supplement* in 1983 asked all heads of departments in four subjects, one of which was Politics, to rank all departments by points for 'Research' and 'Teaching' (terms which were left undefined). We list those which got more than six points.

These scores are probably meaningful in the top range but get pretty random and arbitrary lower down – people simply don't know enough other departments well. And even at the top one suspects some bias or self-validation since the majority of these 'heads' would have done their own postgraduate work a generation ago at one of the three large postgraduate schools, Oxford, LSE or Manchester. The consensus on 'Research' is nevertheless remarkable, and the far wider scatter of opinions on 'Teaching' may hearten the average punter.

Research Rank		*Teaching Rank*	
Oxford	104	Oxford	63
Manchester	77	Manchester	52
LSE	77	Exeter	37
Essex	76	LSE	25
Strathclyde	47	Hull	23
Hull	26	Warwick	14
Warwick	17	Keele	14
Cambridge	10	Reading	14
Exeter	9	Essex	13
Lancaster	6	Lancaster	12
		Cambridge	11
		Newcastle	10
		Leeds	9
		Leicester	7
		Strathclyde	7
		Durham	6
		Sussex	6
		N. Staffs. Poly	6
		Wolverhampton Poly	6
		Edinburgh	6

And the following were 'also rans' in the 'Teaching' stakes: Open University, Leicester Poly, Sheffield Poly, York, East Anglia and Oxford Poly (all rank 5); Southampton, Bristol, Sheffield and Nottingham (all 4); Aberdeen, Liverpool and Kingston Poly (all 3); Brunel, Kent, Glasgow and Birmingham (all 2); and Stirling (1).

Source: *The Times Higher Educational Supplement*, 5 Aug. 1983

Appendix D: Career prospects

There's no denying, however good (or bad) the actual department, that the general repute of the place counts for something in employers' eyes, just as the class of a degree may count for more than the precise subject. In 1986 *The Sunday Times* asked over 500 employers from where they preferred to draw their graduate intake. These were the results (as reprinted in the *The Times Higher Educational Supplement*, 9 May 1986).

Employers' Preferred Institution Across All Subjects

	Universities	*Polytechnics*
1	Oxford	Kingston
2	Cambridge	Bristol
3	London	Coventry
4	Bristol	City of London

5	Manchester	N. Staffs.
6	Durham	Leicester
7	Leeds	Hatfield
8	Exeter	Birmingham
9	Birmingham	Manchester
10	Hull	{ Newcastle Oxford

Employers' Preferences if Social Science Graduates

	Universities	*Polytechnics*
1	Warwick	Glasgow Coll. of Tech.
2	Bath	Bristol
3	Cambridge	Central London
4	Hull	Paisley
5	Oxford	S. Bank
6	Bristol	Oxford
7	Durham	
8	London	
9	Glasgow	
10	Liverpool	

(The difficulty with interpreting this second part of the survey is that some of the answers suggest that by 'social science' some employers simply mean Economics.)

Career patterns from some typical politics departments We were able to collect reasonably comparable figures of the 'first jobs' of 1985 graduates from eight university departments: Birmingham, Durham, Exeter, Keele, Newcastle, Sheffield, St Andrews and Swansea. We simply give totals. It may not be a representative sample at all. St Andrews had an unusually high proportion going into accountancy, Durham into postgraduate studies and legal training, and Keele also legal training. Some of the unskilled jobs are probably temporary while graduates look for something else. But we list them to demonstrate the wide variety. (Those 'believed to be unemployed' about six months after graduation were six per cent of the total in this sample.)

Accountancy	11	Management (& training)	12
Armed services	7	Personnel	5
Banking	8	Police	2
Buying/Marketing/Selling	20	Postgraduate studies	30
Creative arts/Entertainment	4	Public relations & Advertising	5
Civil Service	7	Publishing	3
Clerical	8	Political party officials	2
Computer related	6	Radio/Television	6
Secretarial	3	Research	8
Economic/Statistical work	4	Social services	8
Financial services	19	Shop work	5
Journalism	7	Trade union officials	2
Labouring	4	Believed to be unemployed	13
Legal (& training)	15		

National employment figures for Politics   An official compilation, *University Statistics 1984–85*, identified 893 graduates in Government and Public Administration courses that year of whom the 'career destinations' of 715 were known. Of that number 415 were in employment, 129 in some form of further education or training (53 academic, 15 teacher training and 14 legal), and 130 were 'believed to be unemployed at 31 December 1985'. (This unemployment figure is 14.9 per cent compares to 6 per cent from our departmental sample, which were later returns and therefore more accurate, themselves probably an over-estimate since once people have got a job they tend to loose touch. In any case, graduate employment has improved remarkably since 1985.

Categorized by type of employer the figures are: Public Service 108, Education 16, Industry and Commerce 197 (of which the two largest categories were Accountancy 37, and Banking, Insurance and Finance 49).

Categorized by type of employment the figures are: Administration & Operational Management 82, Scientific Research & Design Development 1, Buying, Marketing & Selling 44, Management Service 11, Financial Work 92, Legal Work 4, Information and Library Work 14, Personnel, Social, Medical & Security Services 52, Teaching and Lecturing 6, Creative & Entertainment 22, and Others 34.

Source: *University Statistics 1984–85: First Destinations of University Graduates* (Universities Statistical Record, Cheltenham, 1986), II, pp. 18–19, 42–3, 66–7.

Appendix E: Some useful books

The UCCA handbook (*UCCA: how to apply for admission to a university*) is essential, it lists courses and is the official explanation of how to apply: *The University Central Council for Admissions Handbook* (PO Box 28, Cheltenham, GL50 IHY).

For polytechnic applications PCAS is the similar official body, see the *Polytechnic Central Admissions System Guide to Applicants* (PO Box 67, Cheltenham, GL50 3AP).

'CRAC' (Careers Research and Advisory Centre) is, of course, a commercial company; its handbooks are not authoritative but are generally of a very high standard. Its *Directory of Further Education* covers the whole range of what is offered in polytechnics and in further education outside the university system (both degree and non-degree courses, including teaching for all those diplomas, certificates and professional qualifications). Specifically useful, especially for more detail on combinations and entrance requirements, is *Politics including International Relations in the UK universities, polytechnics and colleges*, edited by F.E.C. Gregory in CRAC's 'Degree Course Guide' series (Hobsons Ltd, Bateman Street, Cambridge CB2 1LZ).

The Politics Association (chiefly comprising teachers in schools and further education) have a category of student or pupil membership. They run an annual vacation course for A-Level candidates every Easter, and publish the journal *Teaching Politics* and many helpful teaching and study guides. Details can be obtained from the Secretary, The Politics Association, c/o The Hansard Society, 10 Gower Street, London, WC1E 6DP.

There are lots of guides of a general nature on how to get in and how to survive once in, how to live the student life etc., some a bit ucky, but from a wide and uneven field these three may be worth putting a little money on: *The Student Book*, published annually by Macmillan; Peter Wilby, *The Sunday Times Good University Guide* (Granada, 1984) which includes polys and FE colleges; and J.K. Gilbert (ed.), *Staying the Course: how to survive higher education* (Kogan Page, 1984).

Index